Rick Bass

Karsten Heuer

Ted Kerasote

Harvey Locke

Dave Porter

Gary Tabor

Foreword by David Suzuki

Preface by David Quammen

Introduction by Douglas H. Chadwick

Epilogue by Robert F. Kennedy Jr.

yellowstone to yukon freedom to roam

A PHOTOGRAPHIC JOURNEY BY FLORIAN SCHULZ

Published by Braided River, an imprint of The Mountaineers Books, Seattle, Washington
with generous grants from the Yellowstone to Yukon Conservation Initiative and the Campion Foundation

BRAIDED RIVER
CHANGING PERSPECTIVES

An imprint of The Mountaineers Books
1001 SW Klickitat Way, Suite 201, Seattle, WA 98134
www.BraidedRiverBooks.org

Project Manager: Joan Gregory
Acquisition Editors: Helen Cherullo, Deb Easter
Developmental Editors: Deb Easter, Joan Gregory, Linda Gunnarson
Director of Editorial and Production: Kathleen Cubley
Copy Editors: Kris Fulsaas, Alice Copp Smith
Fact Checker: Christine Torgrimson
Cover and Book Design: Ani Rucki
Layout: Ani Rucki
Cartographers: BeesKneesStudioSeattle, Gray Mouse Graphics

All photographs by Florian Schulz except as noted. All images were taken in the Yellowstone to Yukon region, with the exception of some essayist portraits.

Page 1: *Bighorn sheep* (Ovis canadensis) *on the eastern slopes of the Rocky Mountains, Montana.* Pages 2–3: *Sunrise at Lake Sherburn with Mount Wilbur in the background, Waterton-Glacier International Peace Park, Montana.* Title page: *American white pelicans* (Pelecanus erythrorhynchos) *at sunrise.* Dedication page: *Snow geese* (Chen caerulescens) *in flight at Freezeout Lake, Rocky Mountain Front, Montana.* Page 9: *Bison mother* (Bison bison) *with calf on the National Bison Range in Montana.* Page 13: *Lichen on stone, Jasper National Park, Alberta.* Page 23: © *Royalty-Free/Corbis*

Library of Congress Cataloging-in-Publication Data
Yellowstone to Yukon : freedom to roam : a photographic journey / by Florian Schulz ; foreword by David Suzuki ; preface by David Quammen ; epilogue by Robert F. Kennedy, Jr.
        p. cm.
    Includes index.
    ISBN 0-89886-989-7 (hardcover)
    1. Biological diversity—Yellowstone National Park Region. 2. Biological diversity conservation—Yellowstone National Park Region. 3. Biological diversity—Yukon Territory. 4. Biological diversity conservation—YukonTerritory. 5. Biological diversity—Yellowstone National Park Region—Pictorial works. 6. Biological diversity—Yukon Territory—Pictorial works. I. Schulz, Florian.
    QH105.W8Y452 2005
    333.95'16'097875—dc22   2005015799

ISBN 10: 0-89886-989-7
ISBN 13: 978-0-89886-989-7

BRAIDED RIVER—a conservation imprint of THE MOUNTAINEERS BOOKS—combines photography and writing to bring fresh perspective to key environmental issues facing western North America's wildest places. Our books reach beyond the printed page. We take these distinctive voices and visions to a wider audience through lectures, exhibits and multimedia events. Our goal is to inspire and motivate people to support critical conservation efforts and make a definitive difference. Please visit www.BraidedRiverBooks.org for more information on events, exhibits, speakers, and how to contribute to support this work.

THE MOUNTAINEERS, founded in 1906, is a nonprofit outdoor activity and conservation club, whose mission is "to explore, study, preserve, and enjoy the natural beauty of the outdoors. THE MOUNTAINEERS BOOKS supports the club's mission by publishing travel and natural history guides, instructional texts, and works on conservation and history. THE MOUNTAINEERS FOUNDATION is a public foundation established in 1968 to promote the study of mountains, forests and streams of the Pacific Northwest, and contribute to the preservation of its natural beauty and ecological integrity.

Send or call for our catalog of more than 500 outdoor titles:
The Mountaineers Books
1001 SW Klickitat Way, Suite 201
Seattle, WA 98134
800-553-4453
mbooks@mountaineersbooks.org

THE Y2Y PHOTOGRAPHIC PROJECT
BY FLORIAN SCHULZ
WAS MADE POSSIBLE WITH THE GENEROUS
SUPPORT OF

YELLOWSTONE TO YUKON CONSERVATION INITIATIVE

CAMPION FOUNDATION

WILBURFORCE FOUNDATION

ARTHUR B. SCHULTZ FOUNDATION

BLUE EARTH ALLIANCE

KONGSGAARD-GOLDMAN FOUNDATION

GERDA AND ACHIM SCHULZ

SEATTLE FOUNDATION

Canadian Parks and Wilderness Society   Montana Wilderness Association

Craighead Environmental Research Institute   Natural Resources Defense Council

David Suzuki Foundation   The Nature Conservancy

Greater Yellowstone Coalition   United Trust of New York

Dedicated to my wonderful parents, Gerda und Achim Schulz, whose understanding and unconditional support have allowed me to live my dream. I cannot possibly thank you enough!

With love to my partner, Emil, who has graciously dedicated her time and full devotion to assisting me with this magnificent project.

CONTENTS

The Yellowstone to Yukon Ecoregion

- **Actual area:** 460,000 square miles (1.2 million square kilometers), 62% in Canada, 38% in the United States

- **Length:** 1,990 miles (3,207 kilometers), from latitude 42 degrees near Cokeville, Wyoming, to latitude 66 degrees, near the Arctic Circle

- **Width:** Between 125 and 500 miles (202 and 805 kilometers)

- **Height:** Mostly above 3,500 feet (1,067 meters)

- **Highest points:** In the United States: Gannet Peak, Wyoming (13,804 feet/4,209 meters); in Canada: Mount Robson, British Columbia (12,972 feet/3,955 meters)

- **Lowest point:** Mackenzie River, Northwest Territories (200 feet/61 meters)

- **Volcanic features:** Yellowstone, Wyoming: geyser basins; Columbia Plateau, Idaho: lava fields; Mount Edziza, British Columbia: hotsprings

- **Other geological features:** The Rocky Mountain Trench, a continuous line of lowlands extending from central Montana almost to the Yukon, the longest fault system visible on the continent. The Ram Plateau in the Northwest Territories, a major karstland, or formation of soluble limestone, riddled with sinkholes, caves, and sudden canyons. The South Nahanni River area in the Northwest Territories, which includes Canada's deepest canyon (4,000 feet/1,220 meters from top to bottom) and 294-foot (90-meter) Virginia Falls.

- **Major river systems:** Columbia, Missouri, Fraser, Peace, Red Deer, Yellowstone, South Saskatchewan, Athabasca, Mackenzie, Yukon. The Columbia Icefield, the largest glacial mass in the Rockies and the hydrographic apex of North America, sends meltwater to three oceans.

- **Land cover:** 1.5% bare rock, 18.9% tundra, 59% forested, 13.5% shrublands, 4.5% grasslands, 2.6% agricultural. Interior old-growth rainforest along the western slopes of the Rockies.

- **Distinctive wildlife populations:** The continent's most diverse array of large carnivores and densest population of interior grizzlies (found in the Transboundary Flathead area of northwestern Montana and southeasternmost British Columbia). More than 118 fish species. An estimated 10,000 golden eagles and hundreds of bald eagles that migrate annually along the Continental Divide.

- **Indigenous peoples:** Traditional territory of thirty-one First Nation and Native American tribes. Time of continuous human habitation: 10,500-plus years.

- **Current human population:** Less than 3 million. Estimated time until it doubles: 30 to 40 years.

- **Visitor population:** 130 to150 million visitors per day / per year in parks and national forests. Increase in Canada over the past decade: nearly 100%.

- **Land ownership:** More than three-quarters public property—state, provincial, or federal domain

- **Parks and reserves:** Eleven national parks, numerous state and provincial parks, wilderness areas, and ecological reserves. International Biosphere Reserves: Greater Yellowstone area, Waterton-Glacier International Peace Park, Nahanni National Park.

- **Major economic activities:** General tourism, recreation, hunting, fishing, oil and gas, logging, mining

- **Major modern threats to ecosystem continuity:** Backcountry roadbuilding (current road density is 0.21 miles/square mile), highways and railroads, infill of valleys by sprawl, large-scale industrial development, damming and diversion of rivers

- **Solutions to ecosystem fragmentation:** Buffer zones to round out wildland reserves, habitat corridors to keep nature strongholds connected

YELLOWSTONE TO YUKON ECOREGION

Yellowstone to Yukon Ecoregion

National Forest
Forest Reserve — N.F.

National Park
National Park Reserve — N.P.

National Wildlife Refuge
National Wildlife Area
Game Reserve — N.W.R.

Indian Reservation
Indian Reserve — I.R.

Provincial Park — P.P.
Recreation Area — R.A.

Wilderness

Management Area

Highway

ALASKA

ARCTIC NATIONAL WILDLIFE REFUGE

Yukon

Fort Yukon

Inuvik

NUNAVUT

Fairbanks

UNITED STATES
CANADA

Arctic Circle

Peel

Ogilvie
Mountains

PEEL RIVER
PRESERVE

Mackenzie

Tombstone Range

Great
Bear
Lake

Dawson

Yukon

MCARTHUR
WILDLIFE
SANCTUARY

YUKON
TERRITORY

Mackenzie
Mountains

NORTHWEST
TERRITORIES

Pelly Mts.

S. Nahanni

Fort Simpson

Yellowknife

Whitehorse

NISUTLIN
RIVER
DELTA
NATIONAL
WILDLIFE
AREA

NAHANNI
N.P. RESERVE

Great
Slave
Lake

Teslin

Juneau

Cassiar Mts.

Stikine Ranges

Watson Lake

MUSKWA-KECHIKA MANAGEMENT AREA

MUNCHO
LAKE P.P.

STONE
MT. P.P.
WOKKPASH R.A.

Dease Lake

Stikine

Mustwa Ranges

Fort Nelson

NORTHERN
ROCKY MTS. P.P.

DENETIAH P.P.

SPATSIZI
PLATEAU
WILDERNESS
P.P.

KWADACHA WILDERNESS P.P.

ALBERTA

Peace

TATLATUI P.P.

Rocky Mountain Trench

SASKATCHEWAN

Prince Rupert

Dawson Creek

Chetwynd

Mackenzie

Queen
Charlotte
Islands

Fraser

Prince George

KAKWA
P.P.

WILLMORE
WILDERNESS P.P.

North Saskatchewan

PACIFIC OCEAN

Columbia Mountains

MT.
ROBSON
P.P.

JASPER
N.P.

Edmonton

Rocky
Mountains
Forest Reserve

WELLS
GRAY P.P.

YOHO
N.P.

Saskatoon

MT. REVELSTOKE N.P.
Revelstoke

BANFF
N.P.

Fraser

GLACIER
N.P.

MT. ASSINIBOINE P.P.

Canmore

Calgary

Great Plains

BRITISH
COLUMBIA

Rocky Mountain Trench

KOOTENAY N.P.

Invermere

South Saskatchewan

Regina

Vancouver
Island

Kelowna

PURCELL WILDERNESS
CONSERVANCY P.P.
VALHALLA N.P.

Vancouver

Cranbrook

Crowsnest Pass

WATERTON
LAKES N.P.

CANADA
UNITED STATES

Victoria

Columbia

GLACIER
N.P.

Seattle

CABINET MTS.
WILDERNESS

GREAT BEAR WILDERNESS

BOB MARSHALL WILDERNESS

Missouri

Olympia

WASHINGTON

FLATHEAD
I.R.

Fort Benton

MONTANA

Missoula

Portland

Snake

Clearwater

Helena

Yellowstone

Salem

SELWAY
BITTERROOT
WILDERNESS

Bozeman

OREGON

FRANK
CHURCH
RIVER OF
NO RETURN
WILDERNESS

CROW I.R.

Boise

SAWTOOTH
WILDERNESS

RED ROCK
LAKES
N.W.R.

YELLOWSTONE
N.P.

SHOSHONE
N.F.

GRAND
TETON
N.P.

^Gannett Peak

Cokeville

Snake

IDAHO

NAT'L ELK
REFUGE

BRIDGER-
TETON N.F.

CALIF.   NEVADA   UTAH   WYOMING

Great

Green

Laramie

PUBLISHER'S NOTE

THE BROAD EXPANSE OF LAND THAT BEGINS IN YELLOWSTONE NATIONAL PARK and extends along the spine of the Rocky Mountains up and through the Yukon region comprises one of the last fully intact mountain ecosystems on our planet. Yellowstone to Yukon, or Y2Y, is alive with native mammals, birds, and plants in a life-sustaining landscape. The Y2Y Conservation Initiative is the plan that began as a dream of a small group of biologists and conservationists—to link the existing parks in the United States and Canada with connected corridors into one intact ecosystem. This could preserve the habitats of many threatened or endangered wide-ranging and migratory mammals that may otherwise become extinct within decades—including grizzlies and wolves. Fortunately in the case of the Yellowstone to Yukon region, there is still time to piece together the complex solutions to keep this ecosystem intact, but we must act immediately before this slender opportunity slips away forever.

The artistic photographic work of Florian Schulz is a singular and astonishing accomplishment. He has captured the vastness of the region and through imaginative sensitivity reveals the living heartbeat of the web of life that defines it. Florian, a native of Germany, was awestruck at a young age with images of the vast and beautiful wildness and animals of Yellowstone National Park. The seed that became this project was firmly planted, and at twenty years of age he embarked on a journey to capture images of this region that would consume him body and soul for the next ten years. He raised and borrowed funds in order to immerse himself in capturing the remarkable images within this book. This book is his testimony.

Through his travels in other parts of the world, Florian has seen the degradation of nature and knows what a significant treasure we have in our trust. He further envisions the creation of national, state, and provincial corridors—much in the same way as our ancestors over 100 years ago had the foresight to establish national, state, and provincial parks in North America. With this book, Florian also promotes the logical extension of the Y2Y Conservation Initiative to include the Yukon through Alaska to the biological heart of the Arctic National Wildlife Refuge.

Eloquent and generous First Nation, Canadian, and North American essayists who contributed to this book bring a sense of the vastness not only of the landscape but also of the people who live within it. This community of voices affirms in the pages that follow that establishing connections between wild areas need not be paralyzed by partisan politics or disregard for community dialogue. We know that in order for this initiative to be successful, the solution cannot exclude people or rational development within this territory. If it were otherwise, the plan would be doomed to failure before it began. The solutions are also clearly rooted in the premise that an intact ecosystem is by far more valuable than all the natural resources that could be exploited.

This is a visionary plan on all fronts—and perhaps the most ambitious and significant conservation effort in North America today. Through his images of landscapes and wildlife, Florian provides an overview of the life within the Y2Y region that both moves the viewer's heart and supports the science of the vision. If we embrace connectivity and corridors in the Y2Y region, wildlife will continue to have the freedom to roam, and people will become a richly rewarded partner in sustaining this balance.

Helen Cherullo
Publisher, The Mountaineers Books

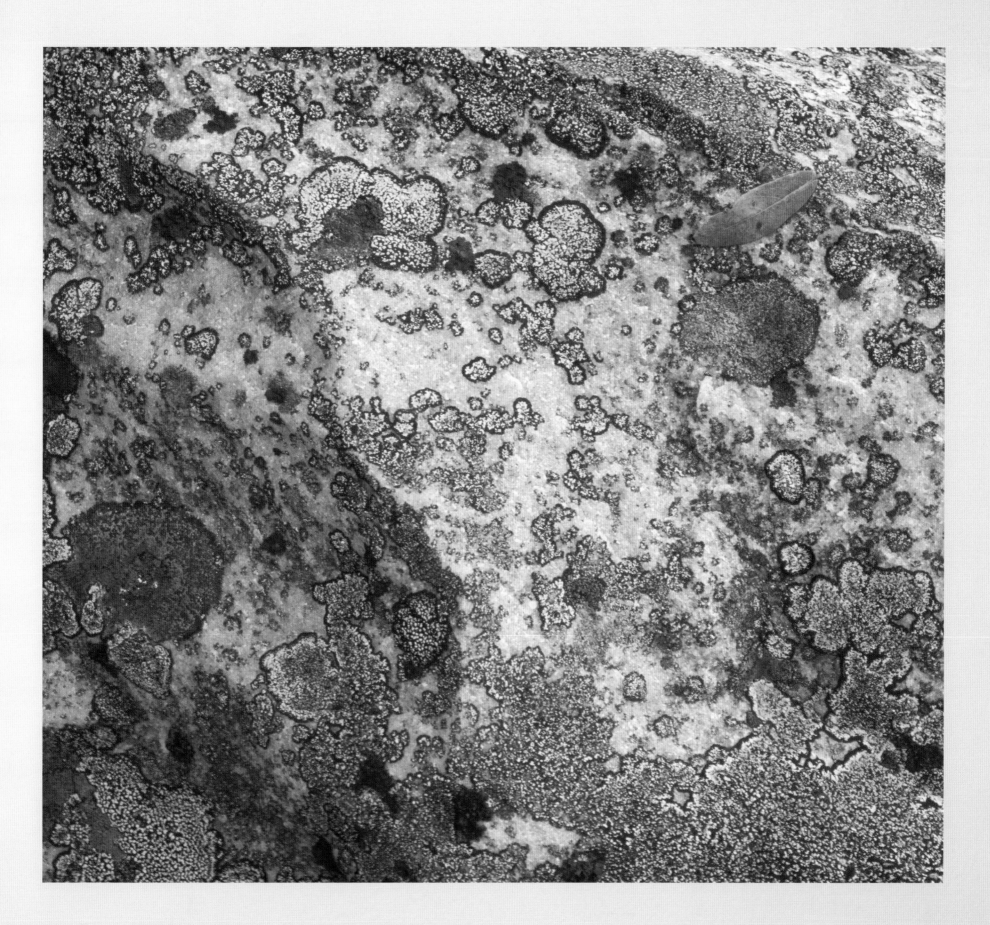

FOLLOWING THE CALL OF THE WILD
Florian Schulz

THERE ARE TIMES WHEN THE WORLD AROUND US BECOMES TOO SMALL, CONTROLLED, and predictable, when our busy modern lives seem to lie so heavily on our chests that we can barely breathe. We want to escape to a place that gives refuge to our souls, where great vistas elevate our spirits, where we can inhale the energy of the landscape.

The Yellowstone to Yukon region is such a place. The Blackfoot call it "the Backbone of the World." People flock here from all over, drawn not only by the magnificent scenery but perhaps even more by the presence of wild animals. As if through a window in history, we can gaze into another time, a world still pulsing with life: bison moving across prairies, wolf packs on the hunt, the bugling calls of elk filling the valleys, river otters fishing the streams, and the mighty grizzly roaming the mountains.

The book that you hold in your hands is an homage to one of the most beautiful wild landscapes left on Earth—the mountain ecosystem of the Northern Rocky Mountains, from Yellowstone to the Yukon: "North America's Wild Heart." Nowhere else in the world will you find such scenic beauty sheltering such a diversity of life. I have been coming to this part of the world for more than ten years. There is something about it that draws me back again and again.

Why would a photographer from Germany spend ten years photographing the Rocky Mountains of North America? There are beautiful mountains in Europe, as well as ancient castles, medieval towns, and ruins that date back millennia. The answer is that we have nothing in Europe that matches the sheer size and scope of the Y2Y area, with its wide-open landscapes and incredible array of wildlife. Most significantly, we don't have true wilderness. We have lost our wildlands. Large wild animals have long since perished. In North America, especially in the vast expanse of the Rocky Mountains, true wilderness still exists. It might be invisible on the surface, but it becomes vividly apparent when one is gazing in awe at a peak such as Mount Assiniboine, and a grizzly with her two cubs walk by. I can guarantee that would never happen at the Matterhorn. The great Rocky Mountain landscapes are a treasure for the world. In them, I see what we in Europe have lost. I don't want that to happen here.

I have been in love with this region for as long as I can remember. As a child, growing up in southern Germany close to Lake Constance and the Alps, I read about the Rocky Mountains and northern regions. Adventure stories by Jack London fueled my imagination, filling my head with visions of a great landscape and its inhabitants. I had my own American dream—not a dream about becoming a millionaire, but a dream about a place where bison herds moved across the plains, grizzly bears roamed the mountainsides, moose browsed the willows, and the howl of the wolf echoed through lonesome valleys.

At the age of sixteen I packed my bags and came to the United States as an exchange student. As soon as I had my high school diploma, I headed for the Canadian Rockies. I still remember staring out the bus window at the mountain walls, looking for a bear behind every boulder. For ten days I hiked through Banff National Park, entranced by the mountains, the lonely valleys, and the wildlife. Finding it difficult to describe what I was seeing to friends and family, I purchased a telephoto lens and photographed my first wildlife shots. That was the beginning of my life as a photographer. I never saw a bear on that first trip, but I knew I would be back—many times.

I returned to Germany and studied biology at the University of Heidelberg for five years. I enjoyed my studies, but the more time I spent in laboratories, the more I realized I had a different calling. I eventually gave up my university career in order to devote

The photographer at Logan Pass, Glacier National Park, Montana (Photograph © by Emil Herrera Jara)

Left: Black bear (Ursus americanus) boar displaying its size with a "thunder walk"

Following page: After the storm, at Many Glacier, Glacier National Park, Montana

15

all of my energy to my passion for photography of wild places. Out in the wilderness, life felt real. Watching Yellowstone National Park change after the reintroduction of the wolves provided an opportunity to study ecology firsthand. I wasn't wearing a lab coat and safety glasses, dropping enzymes into DNA samples that would later be converted to graphs on a computer screen; I was watching natural phenomena reveal themselves in front of my own eyes.

I have since traveled many thousands of miles to several continents, seeking special photographs, unique angles, and light. But making beautiful wildlife and nature images hasn't been my only interest. I have also felt compelled to help protect the environment. And despite the many incredible places I have visited, the Rocky Mountains have always called me back. The Y2Y region has become my second home.

In 2000 I was back in the Rockies doing a story for a German magazine about the endangered grizzly in the Lower 48. During my research, I met scientists such as Dr. Lance Craighead, writers such as Rick Bass, conservationists such as Louisa Willcox, and journalists such as Joel Connelly. The interviews and conversations provided insight into the work of conservation groups in the Yellowstone to Yukon area. I was inspired by their vision. They realize that the isolated islands of national parks and preserves, as important as they are, are not the answer to preserving wilderness or wildlife. We need large, connected stretches of land. Yet in today's world, that is becoming increasingly rare. As Lance Craighead put it, "America is big, but it is not that big. We have another ten, fifteen, maybe twenty years to establish land management plans, set aside land for protection, and establish corridors. If we do not succeed by then, I am not sure how long we will have grizzlies roaming these mountains."

"But," he added, "there is still time to make a difference."

Those are the words that still ring in my ears. I believe the concept of connectivity is extremely important. But we need the general public to support that concept. We need to spread the word as fast as possible. Here I saw a chance to use my skills as a photographer to make a difference. As I talked with scientists and conservationists involved in the Y2Y effort, it became clear—I could create a book about this region. Perhaps sharing my

images would inspire others to get involved in saving North America's greatest treasure.

I developed the concept for the book and approached the Blue Earth Alliance for sponsorship. They accepted. From a small group of encouraging people, the circle of supporters for my project has grown dramatically. The goal has been to create a book that reflects the true glory of the Northern Rocky Mountain landscape and wildlife, displaying the beauty of the land and its creatures. At the same time, it has been important to me to work with writers who have a deep connection to the place and who can write eloquently about their firsthand experiences. Before I even had confirmed a publisher, I had the support of Douglas Chadwick as a contributor, which gave me great energy to carry on. As the project took shape, we were able to win the support of the other writers whose wonderful work you will read on these pages.

I have spent the past five years photographing the Yellowstone to Yukon region exclusively for this project. It has been an enormous task, and not without its challenges and setbacks, both financial and physical. Yet despite the difficulties, I have remained convinced that this project is worth everything I have had to endure to finish it. All the images you see in the book were taken in the wild. I have spent countless hours waiting for those incredible moments to happen. Behind each image is a great, sometimes amazing story. One of the most beautiful aspects of my work has been observing these marvelous animals in their natural surroundings, studying their daily movements, and learning their behavior. Just as in my childhood dreams, I have heard the howl of the wolves and I have watched the grizzlies roaming the mountainsides.

Like the wise people who set aside Yellowstone as the world's first national park in 1872, we need to be visionaries. The vision for Y2Y is a gift that future generations will be able to cherish forever. I want to be a part of the campaign that is making this vision a reality. Through the images of landscapes and wildlife in this book, I hope to paint a picture of the Yellowstone to Yukon region that will move the reader's heart and fuel the new conservation movement of connectivity that will eventually save the Y2Y region for generations to come.

—Florian Schulz

FLORIAN SCHULZ is a professional wildlife and landscape photographer from Germany whose striking images have garnered international recognition. His photographs have won awards in, among others, the BBC Wildlife Photographer of the Year Competition, the Nature's Best International Photography Awards, the Banff International Mountain Photography Competition, and the European Nature Photographer of the Year competition. His stories and photographs have appeared in numerous publications. Schulz spends eight to ten months a year in the field. Images and stories from extended travels through southern Africa and the North American continent are featured in multimedia slide shows. Schulz focuses on environmental and conservation issues and uses his photography to instill in viewers a greater interest in both the natural and cultural diversity of the planet. He has spent a good part of the last decade traveling the Yellowstone to Yukon country to bring back images that he hopes will inspire people to get involved with North America's greatest conservation effort: Yellowstone to Yukon. To view more of his photography, visit his website *www.visionsofthewild.com*.

Idaho's Lemhi Range at sunset

Foggy morning under a bright golden sunrise, Yellowstone National Park, Wyoming

Bison (Bison bison) *grazing in Hayden Valley, Yellowstone National Park, Wyoming*

THE FIRST ASTRONAUTS ON THE WAY TO THE MOON GAVE US OUR MOST stunning icon—a photo of our home seen from outer space. That stunning image captured it all: planet Earth seen as a shining jewel of blue and white set in a backdrop of black, empty space. As space scientist James Lovelock has said, a scientist from another galaxy arriving in our solar system would know instantly that Earth is alive. The high oxygen content of the atmosphere, the stable temperature of the air, and the salinity of the oceans disclose this globe's difference from any other known planet. That picture from space revealed no evidence of the human borders that our species takes so seriously—air, water, and land are all seamlessly held together within the biosphere, providing the underpinning for all life on Earth.

The movements of vast ocean currents, high-altitude atmospheric winds, and dust and topsoil are not constricted by human needs or jurisdictions. Migratory birds and whales moving from South America to the Arctic cannot be claimed by any one country, any more than the elk and wolves that rove across the slopes of the Rocky Mountains can be claimed by the United States or Canada. Nor can the edges of a forest and all its inhabitants be confined within human-made parks or boundaries. Take grizzly bears. In the Lower 48 of the United States, the bears are protected as an endangered species, yet if a grizzly wanders 100 feet (30 meters) across the border into Canada, it can be shot for sport. And grizzlies are known to range over as many as 2,000 miles (3,200 kilometers) of territory.

As astronauts move closer to Earth's surface, the signs of one species—human beings—would leap out. The land is crisscrossed with straight lines of roads, rectangular enclosed farmland, immense lakes backed up behind dams, the checkerboard pattern of clearcuts within forests, and the characteristic brown domes looming above our cities and towns. Human beings have catapulted suddenly into a major force on this planet, capable of altering the biophysical properties of Earth on a geological scale. In the 3.8 billion years of life's existence, no other species has ever had the capacity to do so.

But until the last century, we've always been a tribal animal, living in small family groups of nomadic hunter-gatherers, or more recently in rural, village communities. Under such conditions, our concerns were local, perhaps extending to neighboring tribes or valleys but never encompassing our entire species. Until very recently, we've never had to worry about the collective effect of all of humanity on our surroundings. So now we continue to operate at a local level, much more responsive to anecdotal, personal experience than to the compilation of global statistics. It's difficult to wrap our minds around the immensity of our impact, to think beyond our next paycheck, annual report, or coming election. Yet without paying attention to biogeographical realities, we have no hope of "managing" any organism or ecosystem sustainably.

The challenge is to keep referring back to that picture from space, to remember the oneness of the planet, the need to protect the integrity of that thin web of life that covers Earth, and to recollect our understanding that we are embedded deep within it. Unlike any other organism, we have been endowed with the incredible gift of foresight. By looking ahead, we can anticipate hazard or opportunity and deliberately choose a path into the future. No other species has that gift.

The Y2Y vision of an immense continuous corridor extending from Yellowstone to Yukon and connected to an even wider series of wilderness areas offers a chance to begin that process, to provide a model of what can and must be done all over the planet. Human activity and demand are extending into the furthest reaches of the globe through logging, mining, dams, clearing for agriculture, and urban sprawl. Can human

Left: September in Grand Teton National Park, Wyoming

activity take place while protecting the space and complexity that wild organisms must have in order to flourish? That's the promise of the Y2Y vision.

BIODIVERSITY AS THE SUSTAINER OF LIFE ON EARTH

A truly wondrous aspect of life on Earth is the fact that the fabric of countless interdependent and interacting species—referred to collectively as "biodiversity"—is responsible for creating the oxygen-rich atmosphere, cleansing the water, producing the soil, capturing photons of sunlight, and providing our nourishment. Biodiversity is one of Nature's most successful strategies for resilience and long-term survival. After all, throughout the vast sweep of life's existence on this planet, no "perfect" organism, destined to survive and flourish forever, has ever emerged, because conditions have never been constant or fixed. Change is the hallmark of Earth's history. The Sun is 30 percent hotter than when life began; the atmosphere has become rich in oxygen; magnetic poles have switched; continental plates have moved and collided; ice ages have been punctuated by warm episodes as countless species have evolved and disappeared. All the while, life has persisted and flourished around the planet. The secret to this remarkable resilience is diversity at the gene, species, and ecosystem levels.

Without this diversity, this web of life, the planet would be a hostile place for animals like us. We are absolutely dependent on life's variety to deliver the most fundamental needs we have as biological beings—clean oxygenated air, filtered water, food and the soil for it to grow in, and the Sun's energy for the fuel we burn within and outside our bodies.

We hardly understand how biodiversity carries out these priceless services. However, we've learned from painful and costly lessons in agriculture, forestry, and fisheries that monoculture—the spreading of a single strain or species over a wide area—increases risk through dependence on a limited base that is extremely vulnerable and inflexible when conditions such as new diseases, parasites, or climate shifts arise. So long as there is a pool of diversity, when conditions change there is opportunity for some genes, organisms, or ecosystems to flourish in the new environment. We've also learned that biodiversity is best protected and maintained in large blocks of ocean or land. Restricted to small marine protected areas or terrestrial parks, species continue to decline.

A project like Y2Y provides the dimensions within which diverse life can flourish. It recognizes the need to protect large intact areas in which Nature still functions in all her complexity, not only to cleanse and replenish our basic needs but also to provide us the opportunity to learn her secrets.

HUMAN NATURE AND HUMAN PERCEPTION

For most of our 100,000-year existence, our species, *Homo sapiens sapiens,* lived in an intimate relationship with the natural world. For millennia, we depended on our surroundings for all of our needs, while in that same world we encountered the many hazards of predators, disease, and accidents. Our evolutionary advantage was the most complex structure in the known universe: the human brain. That 4.4-pound (2-kilogram) organ locked inside our skulls endowed us with a relentless curiosity, dazzling inventiveness, and a massive memory. As our distant ancestors gazed out at the world, they recognized cycles and repetitious patterns of day and night, seasons, stages of the moon, movement of stars, tides, animal migration, and plant succession. Those predictable regularities were collected into a worldview, the sum of all observations, insights, and speculations, in which everything, including the past, present, and future, was part of a seamless whole. In such a world of elaborate interconnection, people understood that everything they did had consequences and therefore every deliberate act was laden with responsibility.

Until the most recent century, that is how it always was. Even today, traditional and indigenous people continue to reaffirm that perspective. Their stories, songs, and prayers constantly validate who they are, where they belong on this planet, and why they are here. Aboriginal people often refer to Earth as their mother and say we are created by the four sacred elements: Air, Water, Earth, and Fire. From this perspective, there is no environment "out there," separated from us.

The most advanced insights from science corroborate these ancient truths. Earth *is* our mother, generating all life from air, water, earth, and fire. Air is the physical substance in which we are all embedded and which we share with all other life-forms. It circulates throughout every cell of our bodies and, with each expiration, mixes into the atmosphere and is absorbed by other life-forms. Water is what constitutes more than 60 percent of our body weight; it inflates us and constantly flows through us as it escapes through our skin, breath, tears, and excretions. Like trees and soil microorganisms, we are temporary custodians of the water we imbibe and then release. Every part of our material form, the body, is constructed of molecules and elements scavenged from the carcasses of other life-forms, most of which grew in the soil. And within our bodies, all of the energy that allows us to move, grow, and reproduce is fire from the Sun, miraculously captured by plants and transformed through photosynthesis into stored chemical energy.

Although all human beings are part of a single species, we have found myriad ways of being human. Our cultures reflect the places where people live and the ways we have found to exist within those places. Even though we share the capacity to respond to light, sound, smells, tastes, and textures through a common set of sensory organs and neurological functions, the way we perceive the external world and respond to it is expressed in enormous variety.

Each of us acquires values and beliefs molded by our individual biology, experiences, and environment, and those perceptual lenses filter the input from our sensory organs and thereby shape our reactions and responses. Ethnobotanist Wade Davis explained to me that in a valley in Peru, children grow up believing the mountain looming over their village is an *apu*, or god—not a symbol of god but an actual god—and that so long as they live in the shadow of that *apu*, their destiny is determined. We can be sure that as adults, those children will treat that mountain very differently from people who grow up in the Rocky Mountains believing the surrounding hillsides are laden with valuable minerals just waiting to be exploited. And so it goes. Consider how differently we would behave if to us a forest was a sacred grove, not only timber and pulp; if a river was the veins of the land, not simply water for irrigation or power; if fish were our relatives, not merely resources; if soil was a community of organisms, not just dirt. The way we perceive the world shapes the way we behave toward it.

Sunset in the Lamar Valley, Yellowstone National Park, Wyoming

Left: Tree reflections

A SHATTERED WORLD

In the past century, that world of interconnection, filled with sacred elements and other species that are our biological relatives, has been shattered into fragments that have become, in our eyes, potential resources, wealth, and opportunity. Yet large, intact landmasses provide a reference base against which to measure and recognize the impact of human activity. We cannot deal with the terrible consequences of the fragmentation of our images of the world unless we understand the underlying root causes. Our surroundings have suddenly become a mosaic of disconnected bits and pieces through the conjunction of a number of factors, including population explosion, growth of science and technology, the move from villages and towns to big cities, globalization of the world economy, hyperconsumption, and massive expansion in information.

The first and foremost factor underlying the fragmentation of our perceptions is the population explosion. It took almost all of human existence for the world population to finally reach a billion people early in the nineteenth century; in my lifetime, global population has tripled. One consequence of such explosive exponential growth is that most people alive today have never known anything different and erroneously believe that such abnormal and completely unsustainable growth can be maintained.

Another phenomenon of our recent century is the explosion of science in our lives and its effect on how we perceive the world. Virtually all the modern technology we take for granted in our lives was invented in the past century, each innovation transforming our lives, altering patterns of thought and behavior, and extinguishing the way we lived before. But most scientists today acquire insights by focusing on parts of Nature, instead of on the whole. And we have learned painfully—with nuclear weapons, DDT, CFCs, and biotechnology—that when parts are combined, they interact to yield new properties that cannot be predicted on the basis of the properties of the parts. As well, by focusing only on parts, we lose sight of the context within which they exist, the rhythms and patterns of which they are a part, and the synergy of their interaction.

has created an endless market, while buying, using up, discarding, and buying more have became a way of life and the main part of the economy.

Finally, today's glut of information makes it more, not less, difficult to understand our world. The average person is overwhelmed with information that comes from the print media, the Internet, television, radio, and movies. The challenge is not to acquire yet more information but to navigate these crowded waters, to know what is credible and what is propaganda, self-interest, or advertising. When "I read it" or "I saw it on TV" is all it takes to validate the repetition of some tidbit as fact, we are in deep trouble.

Taken all together, these factors—population explosion, growth of science and technology, the move from villages and towns to big cities, globalization of the world economy, hyperconsumption, and the information explosion—prevent us from seeing the exquisite interconnections that underlie the real world of which we remain a part. In a shattered world of no connections, there are no causal relationships and it becomes difficult to see how our actions ramify through the rest of the world. And when we are blind to cause and effect, we can no longer see where there is a need for responsibility.

Human beings and our activities are undercutting the life-support systems of the planet. We are altering the atmosphere; poisoning air, water, and soil; depleting topsoil and the oceans; clearing forests; and extinguishing species, all at catastrophic rates. It is undeniable that we are careening along an unsustainable path.

AN ANCIENT VISION FOR A NEW WORLD

The challenge of our time is to rediscover hard-earned ancient truths and recognize that as biological beings, we remain utterly dependent on the natural world for our most elementary needs—clean air, clean water, clean soil, clean energy, and a rich diversity of life-forms to keep the planet habitable. Aboriginal people are right—Earth does give us birth, and creates us from the four sacred elements of Air, Water, Earth, and Fire. And we are immersed within a community of our relatives who nourish each other by creating, cleansing, and replenishing those sacred elements. How can we learn these truths without the opportunity to experience the vast expanse of intact Nature?

If we as a species hope to be more than a flash in the pan, making a spectacular splash for a brief moment, then we must resurrect those old understandings, find our place in a world already radically diminished by our own activities and demands. It won't be easy. The past century has witnessed spectacular technological achievements and growth in human numbers and consumptive demand, but modern science is also revealing the illusory nature of this "progress," which has been achieved at the expense of our relatives and a future for our offspring.

Humility would be a good beginning, an acknowledgment of the vastness of our ignorance that in no way detracts from the spectacular insights made in science but merely puts them into perspective with the enormity of our ignorance. Respect for Nature is necessary before we will learn anything or before Nature will open her secrets to us. Love of our children is intimately connected to our love of Nature. And we need Spirit—a sense that we arose out of the natural world and will return to it upon our deaths, that there are forces impinging on us that are beyond understanding or control, that there

As human beings, we have also undergone a remarkable transition in the way we live. Most people on Earth now live in large cities, where our link with Nature is much more tenuous than it was in rural village communities. In such human-created habitats, it is easy to think we don't need Nature, that our intelligence enables us to escape its constraints and create our surroundings.

A fourth factor endangering our connection to and understanding of Nature is the globalization of the world economy. This "global economy," being sold as the key to progress, is fundamentally flawed, its growth inevitably destructive of local communities and local ecosystems. Economists now consider human creativity and inventiveness the very foundation upon which economies are built and view Nature—from the ozone layer and aquifers of fossil water to topsoil and biodiversity—as vast and endlessly self-renewing "externalities" that needn't be factored into economic equations. In such a grotesquely distorted view of the world, the entire planet is viewed as an endless source of raw materials, while all 6 billion of us represent a possible market for the products created from those resources, fueling the economy.

"Newer, bigger, and more" seem to be the driving imperatives of our time. After World War II, the President's Council of Economic Advisors was challenged to come up with a way to transform a war economy to a peacetime economy. Its answer? Consumption. By incorporating disposability and obsolescence into products, industry

The spine of the continent, southwestern British Columbia. Left: The four sacred elements: Air, Earth, Fire, and Water

are sacred places where we must go with veneration to recharge ourselves spiritually. Enlightened self-interest ought to be a prime motivator. Where miners once took canaries into mines as early signals of degenerating air quality, our own children have become canaries, warning us with epidemic levels of asthma, allergies, and childhood cancers.

Four billion years have honed interconnections and interdependencies that we barely comprehend but on which our survival depends. Rather than celebrating the apparent submission of nature to the brute power of our technology, we would be far less destructive, and perhaps find genuine secrets of sustainability, by honoring Nature and hoping she will reveal secrets that we might try to understand and emulate—an approach author Janine Benyus has called "biomimicry."

But we can't learn from Nature unless she is intact. We cannot learn how a system works by simply examining small, isolated patches, any more than we could find out how our bodies function simply by studying its parts separately. Nature needs space and time. But most parks in the world are too small to maintain a stable mix of species or to avoid a continued depletion of diversity. As the climate warms, the species mix within the boundaries of parks will undergo radical shifts: Temperature-tolerant species will persist, while those that are temperature-sensitive will have to move if they are to stay within their range of viability.

The wisest move on our part would be to recognize the enormity of the changes we have already brought about and to begin a massive enterprise, every bit as urgent and vast as entry into a world war, only this time to protect the biodiversity that is the source of our real basic needs. That means we have to aim at bringing our industrial power and productivity, consumption, and numbers into balance with Earth's regenerative capacity. We have to protect every bit of wilderness and intact ecosystems that are left. And we have to begin to connect the disparate patches we call parks or preserves into large communicating areas.

This is the context within which I see the Y2Y project: the beginning of a re-envisioning of our home and our relationship with the rest of life on Earth.

DAVID SUZUKI

Dr. David Suzuki, a highly acclaimed geneticist and environmental thinker, is the author of forty books, including *The Sacred Balance: Rediscovering Our Place in Nature*. He has won numerous academic awards and holds sixteen honorary degrees in Canada, the United States, and Australia. Since 1979, he has been host of the Canadian television series *The Nature of Things with David Suzuki,* for which he has won four Gemini Awards. Recognized as a world leader in sustainable ecology, he is the recipient of UNESCO's Kalinga Prize for Science, the United Nations Environment Program Medal, and the Global 500, and is a member of the Royal Society of Canada and the Order of Canada. He is founder and chair of the David Suzuki Foundation and is professor emeritus of the University of British Columbia, Sustainable Development Research Institute. He lives in Vancouver, British Columbia.

Clypsedra Geyser at sunset, Yellowstone National Park, Wyoming

Yellowstone River in Hayden Valley, Yellowstone National Park, Wyoming

PREFACE

David Quammen

ALMOST FORTY YEARS AGO, IN 1967, TWO YOUNG BIOLOGISTS PUBLISHED A drab little book filled with mathematical equations, schematic diagrams, swooping curves on coordinate graphs, and careful deductions, all grounded in field data from places like Trinidad, Bali, and Krakatau. It wasn't natural history in any old-fashioned sense. It was a technical monograph aimed at other biologists, especially those with a bent toward theoretical modeling and an appetite for calculus. But it triggered a major shift in perspective within the science of ecology, during the 1970s and later, that led not just toward new ideas but also toward urgent actions, including the founding of what we now call conservation biology. From that little book, and from work by other ecologists (such as Michael Soulé, Jared Diamond, Daniel Simberloff, Michael Gilpin, Thomas Lovejoy, Mark Shaffer, and many others) that it inspired, came important implications—some general, some specific—for the design and management of nature reserves, national parks, and other wild lands. One of those implications is that the Y2Y Conservation Initiative is utterly crucial to the fate of species and ecosystems in western North America.

That book was *The Theory of Island Biogeography,* by Robert H. MacArthur and Edward O. Wilson. MacArthur was a mathematical wizard who had done his early ecological fieldwork on warblers. Wilson was a myrmecologist—an ant guy—with a good eye for the number of bristles on a thorax and a good head for bigger ideas. On the first page of their book, they noted that insular biogeography—the study of species distribution on islands—has played a huge role in the development of evolutionary theory, ever since Charles Darwin stepped ashore in the Galápagos. Why? Because islands are simple units that offer stark illustrations of dynamic principles. Two principles in particular interested MacArthur and Wilson: that new species arrive on an island by immigration, and that resident species are lost by extinction. The point of their theory was to explain how those principles function, interact, and thereby determine the biological richness of any given island.

But the two men were talking about "islands," not just islands. Any isolated piece of landscape or water, they noted, is subject to insular principles too. A tide pool, a cave, a stretch of riparian vegetation, a patch of northern forest surrounded by tundra? Yes, these are *ecological* islands, also governed by island dynamics. Then MacArthur and Wilson went a step further, adding a grim warning couched in cool language: "The same principles apply, and will apply to an accelerating extent in the future, to formerly continuous natural habitats now being broken up by the encroachment of civilization." We humans create islands, they were saying, as we cut and bulldoze and pave. By way of illustration, MacArthur and Wilson offered four tiny maps, like a cartoon-panel sequence, showing the loss and fragmentation of woodland in one Wisconsin township over a time span of 119 years. What had been a "mainland" of forest in 1831 was reduced to a sparse "archipelago" by 1950. It was a modest example but a vivid one. Exactly the same process of loss and fragmentation could happen—but must not be allowed to—throughout the magnificent landscapes from Yellowstone to the Yukon.

What's so dire about insularity? What's so crucial about its antithesis, the preservation of landscape connectedness? The answer to that is measured in species diversity and ecological health. A small island usually harbors fewer species than a big island. (This is empirical fact, manifest in field data from the Caribbean, Melanesia, and elsewhere.) A big island harbors fewer species than *an equal area of similar habitat* on a mainland. Why? One major reason, as explained by MacArthur and Wilson, is that small islands tend to lose species more quickly than big islands do, while big islands

Glacier lily (Erythronium grandiflorum) (Photograph © by Emil Herrera Jara)

Left: Grizzly bear (Ursus arctos) *with part of a root in its mouth*

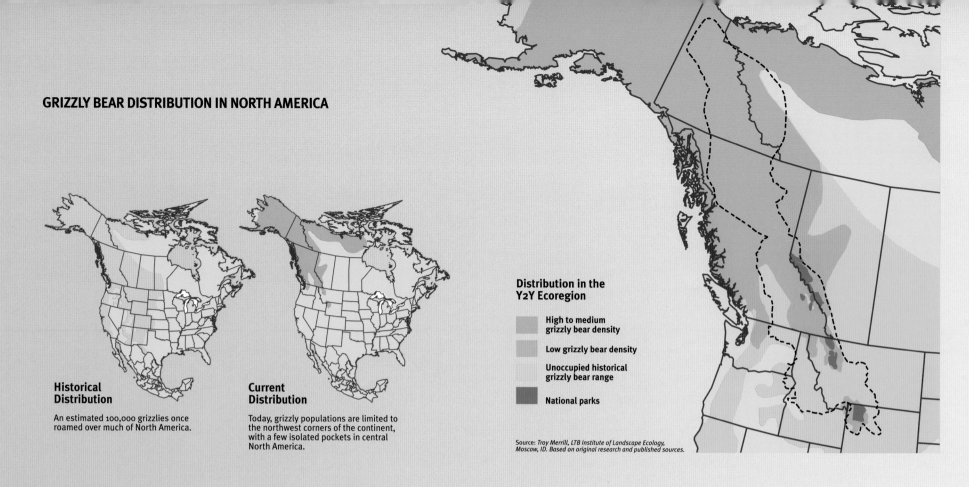

GRIZZLY BEAR DISTRIBUTION IN NORTH AMERICA

Historical Distribution

An estimated 100,000 grizzlies once roamed over much of North America.

Current Distribution

Today, grizzly populations are limited to the northwest corners of the continent, with a few isolated pockets in central North America.

Distribution in the Y2Y Ecoregion

High to medium grizzly bear density

Low grizzly bear density

Unoccupied historical grizzly bear range

National parks

Source: Troy Merrill, LTB Institute of Landscape Ecology, Moscow, ID. Based on original research and published sources.

lose species more quickly than mainlands do. And why is that? Because a small island can support only a small population of, say, this species of reptile or that species of bird; a small population is more vulnerable to the various sorts of adversity (such as inbreeding depression, disease, climate change, food-supply failure, or competition from invasive species) that might wipe it out; and such wipeouts occur inevitably with the passage of time. Small populations go extinct under circumstances in which big populations merely fluctuate. Isolated populations go extinct under circumstances in which mainland populations refill the gaps. Net result: Fragmentation of habitat into ecological islands leads to loss of diversity in each fragment. Loss of diversity leads to ramifying dysfunction of a sort sometimes referred to as "ecosystem decay." Trophic levels begin to wobble and tip. Things fall apart. The disappearance of a predator species, for example, may allow a population explosion among a prey species, resulting in depletion of plant resources, erosion, siltation, and destruction or loss elsewhere in the ecosystem. Maintaining connectedness does the opposite, helping preserve species diversity and ecosystem integrity throughout the whole.

This is abstract stuff. Theoretical talk, hypothetical scenarios. Now let's make it concrete. The grizzly bear (as we call *Ursus arctos* in western North America) is one species that stands sorely jeopardized by the prospect of increasing insularity.

If you look at a map of grizzly bear distribution in 1920, as reconstructed from reliable sources, you'll see small, isolated populations in central Arizona, western New Mexico, southwestern Utah, the southern Sierra Nevada of California, and along the spine of the Rockies in Colorado. All those populations are now gone. Defunct, dead. They vanished, one by one, as a result of island effects and other factors (such as hunting). Nowadays, within the Lower 48 states, grizzlies survive in just five areas: the Greater Yellowstone Ecosystem, the Northern Continental Divide ecosystem around

Glacier National Park, the Cabinet-Yaak ecosystem in extreme northwestern Montana, the Selkirk Mountains of northern Idaho, and the North Cascade Mountains of Washington. Of those areas, all but the North Cascades are embraced within the Y2Y zone of attention. But the Selkirks (harboring no more than a few dozen bears) and the Cabinet-Yaak (with only about twenty) are perilously circumscribed by roads, logging, and other forms of landscape conversion, with further activities looming that could isolate them completely. And the Greater Yellowstone Ecosystem, the southern linchpin of the Y2Y concept, is already an island as far as grizzly bears are concerned—an island on which somewhere between 300 and 600 grizzlies are marooned.

Is the Yellowstone population sufficiently large to sustain itself indefinitely against those troubles I mentioned—inbreeding, food-supply failure, and other forms of catastrophic bad luck? Probably not. With continued isolation on its ecological island (which grows ever smaller as human incursions proceed), the Yellowstone grizzly will be squeezed toward extinction. It might last a hundred years. Or it might founder and die out within this century. And yet the U.S. Fish and Wildlife Service, based on tenuous calculations of what constitutes "recovery" of that population, now seems intent on "de-listing" Yellowstone's grizzlies—that is, removing them from protection under the Endangered Species Act. Can the population *ever* recover so long as it's trapped within Yellowstone Island? I don't see how.

This isn't the place for a discussion of bear-management policy and politics. My purpose is simpler: to sketch a problem, welcoming you to contemplate its solution. In the following pages you'll find hope, beauty, vision, practical wisdom, and not a single differential equation. You'll find a wondrous collection of images and voices. Most important, you'll find new grounds for appreciating a truth that transcends mathematics: that sometimes the whole is much bigger than the sum of its parts.

Grizzly bear (Ursus arctos) *roaming the backcountry of Yellowstone National Park, Wyoming*

DAVID QUAMMEN

David Quammen travels on assignment for *Harper's, National Geographic,* and other magazines, most often to jungles, deserts, and swamps. His accustomed beat is the world of field biology, ecology, evolutionary biology, and conservation, though he also occasionally writes about travel, history, and outdoor sports. For fifteen years, from the early 1980s to the mid-'90s, he wrote a column called "Natural Acts" for *Outside Magazine.* He has received the National Magazine Award three times, and his work has appeared in anthologies such as *The Best American Essays, The Best American Travel Writing,* and *American Short Story Masterpieces.* His books include *The Song of the Dodo,* which won the John Burroughs Medal for nature writing and several other awards; *Monster of God;* and a spy novel, *The Soul of Viktor Tronko.* He lives in Montana with his wife (Betsy Gaines, a conservationist), their large furry dog, and a modest supply of cats.

YELLOWSTONE GRIZZLY.   For several years I have observed this beautiful grizzly. Her distinctive face makes it easy for

me to recognize her. Sometimes she roams the Swan Lake Flats of Yellowstone National Park. This was the first time I had seen

her this year. With my binoculars, I watched her move nose down through the wet sagebrush. Then I realized she was not alone!

Two cubs were by her side, still so tiny they kept disappearing into the brush.

When the mother raised her head to look around, one of the cubs imitated her, standing on tiny hind legs to peer over

the dense brush. The mother found an anthill and started digging into it. The cubs immediately joined in.

In the coming months, the cubs will mimic every move their mother makes. There is so much to learn in this harsh climate,

and enough food is the key to survival. The mother grizzly will teach her cubs where to find white-bark pine seeds, where to

dig up ground squirrels, and what roots to eat.

I watched and photographed this grizzly family until they

wandered away over the hillside. Decades of protection under

the Endangered Species Act have made such observations

possible. To me, this bear family is an encouraging sign for

the future of grizzlies in Yellowstone. I can only hope they

will remain protected beyond park borders.

—F.S.

Yellowstone grizzly bear (Ursus arctos) *and cubs*

Mount Assiniboine at sunrise, Assiniboine Provincial Park, British Columbia

THE HEART, THEY SAY, IS THE MOST RUGGED, ENDURING MUSCLE A HUMAN possesses. It has to be to keep pumping life force through the rest of the body year after year, decade after decade, without fail. There is a region of the Rocky Mountains that manifests many of the same qualities—a fount of natural power from which vitality pulses out to animate the surrounding lands. In the quiet among the peaks, you can almost hear each beat. This is North America's great wild heart, and the challenge of the modern era is to keep it from breaking.

YELLOWSTONE

Ninety-six years after the United States came into being, its legislators drew a boundary around 3,600 square miles (9,300 square kilometers) at the juncture of Wyoming, Montana, and Idaho. Of course, those miles weren't actually square. They were rough-edged, river-cut, beautifully bent and tilted, and more than a mile high on average, erupting with geologic marvels and wildlife splendor to match. Let us, the politicians said, keep this place as it is. Forever. The year was 1872. They were establishing Yellowstone as a national park, the first in the country and in the world.

Underlying this act was a recognition that an age of vanishing herds and forests was all too suddenly upon the young republic, and that the time for measuring its natural resources solely as raw materials had passed. People need riches that can be banked in the heart. They need natural beauty and wonder. They need hope and inspiration, and they need a sense of their heritage, their identity, which in the case of North America's populace is bound to an untamed frontier. Of what use are all the blessings of a free society if the blessings that Nature has bestowed upon the landscape are lost? A nation risks becoming merely a location where people go about the business of existing, as in a sleep without dreams. Yellowstone National Park was a gift from a popularly elected government to its citizens and all their descendants, intended as a boon for their souls.

The setting aside of wildlands as public parkland created a new type of commons. History had never before seen such a generous blend of nature and democratic ideals. Canada quickly adopted the innovation, framing Banff National Park farther north along the Rockies in western Alberta as early as 1885 and Waterton Lakes National Park next to the Montana border in 1895. Other countries followed all through the next century, and the process continues today around the globe. Together, these areas have become modern strongholds for many of the most vital aspects of nature that renew the human spirit as well as the ecosystems we all depend upon.

YUKON

More than a thousand miles to the north of Yellowstone begins a Canadian expanse of 320,000 square miles (829,000 square kilometers) with fewer than 40,000 people. This is the Yukon Territory, and the great bulk of it remains undisturbed by roads or major developments, nearly as pristine as it was on the day Yellowstone was declared a national park. What comes next? A few segments have been permanently protected as parks, territorial reserves, or wildlife refuges. More may follow. But must we assume that the rest of the Yukon will eventually repeat the history of realms farther south, where so much of the natural legacy that people once enjoyed has been shoved into corners or lost?

Perhaps if we build on the example of Yellowstone, progress will once again be

INTRODUCTION
Y2Y: The Power of Connections

Douglas H. Chadwick

Northern pintail ducks (Anas acuta) *during migration*

Left: The Columbia River and Columbian Wetlands at sunset, British Columbia

defined differently before the Yukon is largely given over to development. What if the goal were not to divide up the territory between commercial activities and scattered samples of the former landscape but to interweave human and wild communities within the context of a unique and lasting frontier? What if this same principle were applied to the great north-south coalition of mountain terrain that surges all the way between the Yukon and the world's first national park?

YELLOWSTONE TO YUKON

The essence of nature is wholeness—a wholeness woven from infinite complexity. Trying to save it piece by piece doesn't really make much sense. That strategy wouldn't work even if we had all the time in the world, and we most certainly do not. Overall biological diversity (the full spectrum of native organisms and ecosystems, plus all the processes and interactions associated with them) is plummeting at a rate not seen since the dinosaurs' demise.

Yet it was late in the twentieth century before the realization spread among scientists that traditional approaches to conservation were far too fragmentary, too tightly focused on special areas or individual species in crisis, to shore up the natural systems that were under assault. Grass-roots environmental groups felt the same way, for they found themselves bogged down in divisive local debates over single issues while they faced multiple problems on a wider front.

The longer researchers followed wildlife marked for study in Yellowstone National Park, for instance, the more they found their subjects using a wildland mosaic nearly ten times as big as the reserve itself. To its wild inhabitants, the famed park was merely one room of their true home, which came to be recognized as the Greater Yellowstone Ecosystem. All through the Rockies, planners were assembling larger-scale maps and starting to analyze entire countrysides, watersheds, and plant and animal communities from a new perspective. They spoke of each node or nucleus or central swath of wildlands as a core. Then they looked for buffer zones, surrounding lands that might host certain human activities but would insulate the pristine core from acreage with still higher levels of disturbance. Going further, the planners identified pathways of intact ground leading from one core area to the next. Here were the system's linkage zones, more commonly called wildlife corridors or habitat bridges. In the end, what emerged was a pattern of hope.

During the mid-1990s, ecologists and conservationists gathered in Waterton Lakes National Park, Alberta, to share their evolving ideas. Between that conclave and follow-up meetings, a proposal for safeguarding biological diversity and natural beauty was conceived on a scale beyond anything tried in North America—or, one could claim, in the world. Quickly winning the support of more than 120 organizations (the number has since grown to more than 200) from Canada and the United States, this strategy addressed close to half a million square miles (1.3 million square kilometers) along nearly 2,000 miles (3,200 kilometers) of the Continental Divide, from west-central Wyoming to the Yukon's Peel River near the Arctic Circle, and from the edge of the Great Plains halfway to the Pacific Coast. Its name is the Yellowstone to Yukon Conservation Initiative.

Grizzly bear (Ursus arctos) *eating western serviceberries* (Amelanchier alnifolia)

Left: Kintla Lake, Glacier National Park, Montana

It has often been said that the national park system of public lands is the best idea America ever had. Y2Y (as people now refer to both the Initiative and the area) takes the concept to the next level. You could call it the rest of the best idea. This does not imply that Y2Y is a plan for some all-encompassing park, despite rumors to the contrary. The region already has eleven national parks, scores of state parks, provincial parks, and designated wildernesses, and many other relatively unspoiled areas under special management. These are nature strongholds of global significance. But they are not as strong as they need to be.

Wild species have to move around freely and mingle with others of their kind to adapt to shifting conditions over time and to avoid inbreeding, which can lead to local extinction if enough deleterious traits become concentrated in the gene pool. None of the reserves in Y2Y is big or complete enough by itself to provide this sort of ecological wriggle room. Consequently, none will be able to support its full endowment of biological diversity through the years, which means that none can truly fulfill its purpose as a sanctuary. On the positive side, a cure for the problem lies in links with other wildlands, and Y2Y is all about the power of connections.

The initiative's first aim is to round out the region's extraordinary collection of protected places with necessary buffer zones and fasten the whole assemblage together through habitat bridges. The broader and more varied the linkages, the better, such as the series of mountain valleys wolves follow when traveling between Banff National Park and Montana's Glacier National Park. But where a narrow, winding, green strip is all that

will fit through a bottleneck of development, it can still serve, like the thick streamside brush grizzlies use for cover when moving between open agricultural fields.

Once such a network is in place, step number two is to combine it with a plan for sustainable use of natural resources in adjoining landscapes. Carefully managed recreation would be one obvious type of compatible development. Or, instead of clearcutting forests and shipping the raw logs off to distant mills, or even to other continents, timber companies could practice selective cutting and thinning to leave much of the forest structure intact and mill the logs into lumber locally, providing extra employment. Then, rather than exporting the wood at that stage, the mills could supply area businesses set up to manufacture distinctive regional furniture, frames, specialty trim board, veneers, or a hundred other items that economists term value-added products. These fetch higher prices than raw logs or lumber, and the money stays in the communities where the trees grow.

Forests cover almost 60 percent of the Y2Y region. Not surprisingly, logging has the most widespread impacts on landscapes. Tenbec, a Canadian timber company with worldwide holdings, recently forged a special agreement with The Nature Conservancy of Canada. The corporation sold several thousand acres to the conservancy outright and donated permanent conservation easements (which restrict certain options, notably subdivision for homesites) on several thousand additional acres. Moreover, company officials voluntarily placed a ten-year moratorium on all activities except limited tree cutting on another 89,000 acres and promised to consider renewing the ban after that. This novel pact represents a priceless reprieve for the Elk River watershed in a rapidly developing part of southeastern British Columbia, where the Y2Y region becomes vulnerably narrow near Waterton-Glacier International Peace Park. Tenbec didn't do this for the money. The company's managers said they simply agreed with the principles of conservation.

Doing business in greener directions like this would give people and nature a chance to prosper side by side into the future as the human population of Y2Y— still just a few million within those enormous boundaries—expands. Both a practical strategy and a unifying vision, Y2Y may be thought of as a blueprint for bringing the forces of culture, economics, and ecology into balance. This seems like the most sensible goal in the world. Since it also seems among the hardest to achieve, maybe a better definition for Y2Y is "a much-needed experiment in the grandest of laboratories."

TAKING INVENTORY

Described by some as the backbone of the continent and by others as its wild heart, the area from greater Yellowstone to the Yukon qualifies as a distinct ecoregion, with similar geology, climate, habitats, and native creatures throughout. It comprises North America's tallest, most rugged, and arguably most spectacular unit of topography—an exaltation of the land—and the headwaters for ten major rivers flowing into three different oceans. The dramatic differences in altitude are reflected in the spectrum of vegetation: A morning walk can drop you from wind-scraped alpine tundra lit with miniature forget-me-nots down onto a mushroomy forest floor shaded by cedar giants a thousand years old.

Flathead Valley and logging development in British Columbia; lumbermill at Invermere, British Columbia

Left: Flathead Valley, site of proposed expansion of Waterton-Glacier International Peace Park

CONCENTRATION OF CARNIVORES AND UNGULATES IN NORTH AMERICA

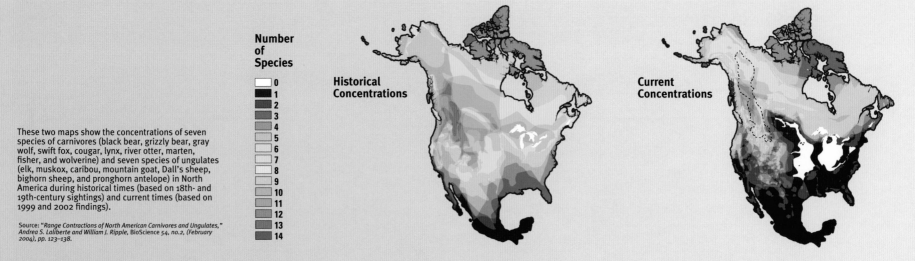

Number of Species

	0
	1
	2
	3
	4
	5
	6
	7
	8
	9
	10
	11
	12
	13
	14

Historical Concentrations

Current Concentrations

These two maps show the concentrations of seven species of carnivores (black bear, grizzly bear, gray wolf, swift fox, cougar, lynx, river otter, marten, fisher, and wolverine) and seven species of ungulates (elk, muskox, caribou, mountain goat, Dall's sheep, bighorn sheep, and pronghorn antelope) in North America during historical times (based on 18th- and 19th-century sightings) and current times (based on 1999 and 2002 findings).

Source: "Range Contractions of North American Carnivores and Ungulates," Andrea S. Laliberte and William J. Ripple, BioScience 54, no.2, (February 2004), pp. 123–138.

And Y2Y's animals…ah, the beasts that give the backcountry eyes. They form the biggest, brawniest, fiercest, shaggiest, longest-legged, far-rambling array in the Western Hemisphere. It's a pleasure just to be able to give the roll call: grizzly, black bear, wolf, coyote, cougar, lynx, wolverine, fisher, otter, mountain goat, mountain sheep, moose, bison, caribou, elk, mule deer, white-tailed deer, golden eagle, bald eagle, osprey, peregrine falcon, prairie falcon, tundra swan, trumpeter swan, sandhill crane, whooping crane, harlequin duck, Pacific giant salamander, tailed frog, chinook salmon, bull trout…. The list goes on. And on, down canyons with free-flowing white waters, up palisades and scree slopes, across glaciers, and on through range upon mountain range. To find a more enthralling collection of megafauna amid megavistas in the New World, you would have to time-travel back to the Ice Ages.

This sweep of rough-and-tumble terrain is also the homeland of more than thirty Native American tribes, or First Nations, as they are called in Canada. Most of them retain a portion of their traditional territory along with subsistence hunting and fishing rights. Few incoming Europeans bothered trying to carve out homesteads from such steep, often snowbound terrain. Less than 3 percent of the region is classified as agricultural land today and less than 8 percent as additional grazing land. By contrast, more than 20 percent is bare rock or tundra. At least three-quarters of the total acreage consists of state or federal lands on the U.S. side and crown land (provincial or federal domain) in Canada. Although native land claims have yet to be resolved in many places north of the international line, the point is that most of Y2Y is the property—the holdings, the inheritance—of the public as a whole.

The fact that the Y2Y region never did exactly get settled, much less crowded, goes a long way toward explaining why every species of megafauna the pioneers met is present today. By twenty-first-century standards, this colossal setting is still largely of a piece. Instead of struggling to make their environment clean and healthy, residents have only, for the most part, to choose to keep it that way. However, development pressures are building as globalized markets and new technologies push industries ever farther into the hinterlands. Open-pit mining to produce coal for China's burgeoning steel industry is planned close to Waterton-Glacier International Peace Park. An ore-mining operation just opened near Alberta's Jasper National Park. Millennium-old interior

cedar-hemlock forests that shelter the increasingly rare race known as mountain caribou are being leveled in British Columbia valleys to supply Asian lumber mills. New grid lines cut for the seismic test blasts used to locate oil and gas reserves run over remote mountainsides. And the list keeps lengthening like the bulldozer trails.

At the same time, a tide of new settlement has begun washing over the mountains' feet. Remote spots that once deterred newcomers are suddenly attracting all kinds of people eager to escape urban areas. A lifestyle with a rural pace and outdoor recreation is the lure for countless others yet to come—especially now that they can keep in touch and do business from almost anywhere via the Internet and satellite dishes.

THINKING LIKE A WOLVERINE

If Y2Y is to win support for securing crucial habitat bridges between wildlands while there is still time, some major gaps must also be bridged between the way people perceive ecosystems and the way they actually operate. This region hosts the most diverse assortment of large carnivores in the Americas. How much room will it take to keep them? In the section of the Rockies where I live, a grizzly's home range may encompass 500 square miles (800 square kilometers) or more. A silvertip met in Glacier National Park, Montana, one day might appear in the Great Bear Wilderness to the south the next week, then ramble east over the Blackfeet Indian Reservation, north into Alberta ranch country, west across the Great Divide into British Columbia, and south again into Montana's Flathead National Forest.

A few years ago, researchers started attaching radio transmitters to wolverines in Glacier National Park. I've spent a lot of days as a volunteer helping to track them but can hardly ever keep up. As it turns out, some males, which weigh all of 30 to 35 pounds (13 to 16 kilograms), roam territories the size of a grizzly's home range. The wolverine labeled M8, radioed near Glacier's eastern edge, ventured west over the Lewis Range and then the Livingston, Whitefish, Salish, and Purcell ranges to take up residence around Montana's common border with Idaho and British Columbia. In the Greater Yellowstone Ecosystem, a different study recently documented a young male wolverine roving 550 miles (885 kilometers) in seven weeks. The line drawn around all

Clockwise from upper left:
golden eagle (Aquila chrysaetos);
western tanager (Piranga ludoviciana);
hoary marmot (Marmota caligata);
white-tailed deer (Odocoileus
virginianus); *red fox* (Vulpes vulpes) *pup;*
bison (Bison bison)

Y2Y CRITICAL CORES AND CORRIDORS

1. Greater Yellowstone Ecosystem
2. Centennial-Tobacco Root-Gravelly Mountains
3. Clark Fork Corridor
4. St. Joe-Coeur d'Alene-Upper Clearwater
5. Salmon-Selway-Bitterroot Mountains
6. Cabinet/Yaak
7. South Selkirk Mountains
8. Northern Continental Divide Ecosystem
9. Northern Crown of the Continent Ecosystem
10. Canadian Rocky Mountain Parks Complex
11. Rocky Mountain Trench
12. Peace River Break
13. Muskwa-Kechika Management Area
14. Upper Liard Basin
15. Greater Nahanni Watershed
16. Wolf Lake Ecosystem
17. Peel Watershed

Source: *Yellowstone to Yukon Conservation Initiative, 2005*

With the help of their research on grizzly bear habitat, the Y2Y Conservation Initiative identified thirteen "Critical Cores and Corridors" (CCCs) that are crucial to the survival of key wildlife species in the Y2Y region. Another four CCCs in the northern region were identified based on information about key watersheds, protected areas, and opportunities for conservation.

its paths encompassed 23,000 square miles (59,600 square kilometers). A lynx radioed in Montana's Swan Valley was later located 250 miles (400 kilometers) north next to British Columbia's Kootenay National Park. Wolves are known to journey between Glacier's parklands and those of Banff, and one female tagged in northwestern Montana showed up in the Yukon. If you think that any park alone is sufficient to meet the needs of predators like these, you have, as they say, another think coming.

So think big. Then think bigger. Aside from the tendency of such animals to just take off and go at times, their normal home ranges or territories are too vast for very many to fit entirely within a reserve. Suppose officials give out an estimate of 100 for some large carnivore in a park. That sounds encouraging. But half may regularly prowl outside the boundaries, exposed to whatever policies prevail there. Besides, if the group lacks contact with others, even twice that many individuals would represent too small a sample to avoid inbreeding. Experts say that for a typical large mammal species, at least 500 reproductive adults—not just 500 animals—are needed to maintain an adequately varied gene pool.

THINKING LIKE AN ELK

With the exception of caribou and bison, vegetarian members of the wildlife community don't typically wander as far and wide as the carnivores do. But the hoofed animals of the Rockies do wander high and low, migrating thousands of vertical feet between seasonal ranges. In some cases, the summering sites lie miles from the wintering grounds. Juveniles may cover considerably greater distances when dispersing to seek homes of their own. Like the meat-eaters, then, the herbivores need their share of elbow room. Finally, predators, prey, and even plants continually shift ranges over generations as they adjust to the effects of avalanches, floods, disease epidemics, insect outbreaks, droughts, wildfires, and climatic cycles. Not to mention global warming.

As is typical for mountainous areas, the boundaries of most reserves within the Y2Y region were established with an emphasis on the highest of the high country, because that's where the gasp-in-awe scenery shines, and because industries seldom objected to setting aside glorious jumbles of rocks and ice that they didn't have much use for anyway. As a result, many a park ends partway down a mountainside—just where temperatures begin to warm and steep rubble gives way to stable soils. From this level down is where the majority of plants thrive and the majority of browsers and grazers want to be during spring to reach the earliest green growth, and again in autumn after the vegetation upslope drops its berries and leaves, and then through the deep winter.

In rugged northern terrain, the warmest, lushest, most sheltered habitats of all stretch along valley floors. Being the flattest habitats as well, they become repositories for soil and nutrients and collectors of moisture in rivers, lakes, and marshes. Life-forms from orchids and currants to nesting birds and calving elk favor the low-lying areas, making them hot spots of biological diversity. However, these bottomlands are at a premium in the Y2Y ecoregion. Hemmed in by sawtooth topography, most of them are fairly narrow and widely separated from the next swath of level ground. They are

A lone gray wolf (Canis lupus) *running through the Lamar Valley, Yellowstone National Park, Wyoming; wolf watchers in Lamar Valley, with Soda Butte Creek in the background*

also the first habitats to fill with people, for we too naturally gravitate to the valleys and neighboring foothills. Their gentle contours speak to us not only of hospitable homesites and livestock pastures but of handy bases for commerce and logical routes for highways and railroad lines.

The past bias toward the subalpine and alpine life zones for reserves is exactly why Y2Y advocates buffer zones to help extend protection to the key seasonal ranges and fertile wetlands below. And the growing competition for limited bottomland acreage is behind the call to secure habitat bridges through valleys before dense development monopolizes them, permanently displacing wildlife communities and cutting off their movements between mountain ranges.

SUPPLY AND DEMAND

Although the Y2Y region remains lightly populated, studies show that its national parks and public forests support more than 130 million visitor days of recreation each year. The count is rocketing upward. Clearly, the Rockies' big heart is providing opportunities for a great many visitors from other places to find whatever it is they seek in wild and beautiful surroundings. How do we measure that? What is the value of Yellowstone National Park today compared to its value in 1872? What will it be in the next century?

Looking at worth in strictly financial terms, considerable revenue is already streaming into the region because it is so well stocked with mountain panoramas, sparkling air and water, majestic creatures, and untamed places to explore. New enterprises and opportunities tied to general tourism, adventure travel, river running, cross-country skiing, hiking and camping, hunting and fishing, world-class wildlife viewing, and similar activities are multiplying like saplings at the edge of a floodplain. And as unspoiled vistas and charismatic wildlife become scarce commodities on an increasingly hard-used planet, a lot more people are going to be willing to pay a lot more money to enjoy the qualities of life stored in Y2Y. Based in the core of two affluent, stable democracies, this region has every chance of emerging as the most intact mountain ecosystem left between the polar latitudes.

The Y2Y area's business model was semicolonial. Raw materials were extracted by outside-owned corporations and shipped from the frontier to more developed areas for processing. Even industries based on renewable resources such as timber were subject to boom-and-bust cycles governed by market forces over which local folks had little or no control. Some would say the situation hasn't changed in many Rocky Mountain outposts. But the Y2Y vision is focused on a more stable, diversified economy. The ideal might be a balance of recreation-oriented operations and traditional industries retooled to avoid exploiting any single resource on a scale that diminishes others.

Yet despite the growing dominance of commerce based on the region's amenities, part of the public continues to view nature protection and economic development as opposing interests: jobs or the environment, opening up the backcountry or locking it away. It's the old-school dogma and hard to overturn. Ironically, many visitors who pass through the region's parks and take in the most magnificent expanses of country they have ever seen in their lives leave convinced that the task of saving nature has more or less been accomplished. They cannot imagine that such immense, craggy fortresses wouldn't serve to guard any number of creatures indefinitely. But the date on that mind-set has expired too.

AS A MATTER OF FACT

Since Yellowstone was declared a national park, the field of biology has added 133 years' worth of discoveries. And the findings are telling us that the notion of parks as outdoor museums where society can tuck flora and fauna away and come back at any time to find each perfectly preserved is quaint as a corset. If anything, trying to protect nature in isolated sanctuaries is a recipe for extinction.

Species are not specimens but dynamic works in progress. Communities are not collections of species so much as mixtures of organic chemicals, genes, instincts, acquired immunities, memories, social behaviors, communication techniques, and niches that are constantly evolving relative to one another. The wonder of nature is found less within individual plants, animals, microbes, or aspects of the physical environment than in the manifold linkages among them. Just as with Y2Y, the real power comes from the connections. Connections such as ravens circling and calling to lead wolves to a carcass so they will open up the tough hide. Or young grizzlies

learning to raid the seed caches made by jays and industrious squirrels. Or the symbiosis of fungi, algae, and, sometimes, bacteria that forms the organisms we call lichens, and the way many lichens live on trees and extract nitrogen from the passing air, supplying as much as half of an old-growth forest's need for this essential element.

Following the prime law of ecology—that everything is ultimately hitched to everything else—the allies of vitality are flux and flow and partnerships. The enemies are the forces that lead to separateness: fragmentation of larger landscapes, fixed borders, and confinement within habitats too small to withstand disruptive forces impinging from outside. Life on Earth, biological diversity, Nature—whichever name you use, it is a whole immeasurably greater than the sum of its parts, and we simply have to get better at seeing it that way in order to save it.

Because the Y2Y Initiative suggested additional conservation measures for certain public lands, some interests criticized it from the start as a threat to local economies. Opposition has been loudest in the United States, though barely more than a third of the total Y2Y area lies south of the international border and this is the portion most fractured and in need of connections. Hearing that the Initiative is controversial, many assume that it must indeed represent a fairly extreme point of view. It does not. It's hardly even an opinion.

Mountain goats, great gangling moose, silver-tipped bears whose footprint alone can change your outlook on the day—creatures of these dimensions didn't arise in leftovers of wild landscapes. Leftovers won't long sustain them or the communities to which they belong. This isn't speculation. It is something learned from studies of genetics; from biogeography, which has shown that the smaller an island is and the farther it lies from a continent's coast, the lower its total number of species; and from documented declines in mainland parks increasingly isolated amid a sea of developed habitats. Facts are facts. Not that you can't still make a choice. If you're serious about conserving the quality of life along the backbone of the continent, look into Y2Y; if you aren't, don't. We have a limited time in which to reinforce the wholeness of nature or condemn ourselves to watching it fade like the embers of a fire that once warmed us. As the quest for industrial commodities closes in on the last backcountry, the rarest, most precious commodity of all will surely be the freedom of the wild.

MADE FRESH DAILY

In contrast to the usual piecemeal approach to land management, Y2Y is a genuinely fresh plan of action. That's particularly fitting because it matches the freshly made, active land whose skyline has been rising for millions of years and continues to inch skyward today. Glaciers and icefields still cut the alpine edges to shape, while plants compete to invade the shavings we call moraines. The subalpine slopes keep coming

Elk herd (Cervus elaphus) *during spring migration in the Greater Yellowstone Ecosystem;* *trumpeter swan* (Cygnus buccinator) *cleaning its feathers*

loose in slumps, rockslides, and avalanches. Waterfalls tumble everywhere. Streams cascade at steep angles. The rivers' waters run in rapids, and the winds washing across North America's heights are strong enough to buffet you like surf. Cloudbanks and storms can materialize all at once and vanish nearly as fast. In motion, overhead and underfoot, the region feels eternally new and full of promise.

When you move beyond the outskirts of Y2Y to where the landscape has found its angle of repose, it begins to run short of surprises, particularly where every contour seems allocated to human pursuits. It is hard to pin down exactly why mountains are so invigorating by comparison. But I know that soaring terrain, soaring eagles, and soaring thoughts go together, just as wholeness in the environment is tied to wholeness in one's self. Time spent among intact landscapes and wildlife communities is potent medicine for a stressed-out era. Enough doses could heal a society.

Now, going into a town of loggers or miners and yakking about how nature knits the pysche together might not win many new friends. Better to discuss how to manage resources in ways that guarantee jobs for their children and grandchildren rather than cycles of overharvesting followed by factory closures. After all, that's part of the Initiative as well.

Humans have been trying to figure out for a very long time who we are and where we are going. The pervasive modern question of how people and their livelihoods can flourish in a place without overloading the environment is part of that long-standing quest. Y2Y offers some meaningful solutions for at least one special section of the world. Progress for its own sake is not really progress. Y2Y is.

The Initiative is also more than the subjects I have introduced so far. It is a staff and volunteers based in Canmore, Alberta, just east of Banff National Park, as well as representatives in other provinces and states. It is funding and coordination for research projects. It is rounds of meetings and symposia. It is a growing atlas with detailed maps of resources, from vegetative cover to the distribution of fish in watersheds to road densities. It is a list of CCCs—Critical Cores and Corridors—that the maps highlight as most in need of immediate attention. It is charts of economic statistics such as per capita income by industry in various districts. It is outreach programs in church basements, complete with slide shows, discussions—and, of course, cookies.

Y2Y is also one of the reasons wildlife overpasses were built over the Trans-Canada Highway that races through Banff National Park, why Bow Valley Wildland Provincial Park and Spray Lakes Provincial Park were recently established next to Banff, and why a 15.6-million-acre mix of wilderness parks and special management areas, jointly known as Muskwa-Kechika, was set aside in northern British Columbia. The initiative is a factor as well in the Canadian federal government's support for expanding Nahanni National Park from a narrow ribbon in the Northwest Territories, and for rounding out Waterton-Glacier International Peace Park by adding a chunk in British Columbia's Flathead Valley, which contains interior Canada's densest grizzly population along with perhaps the single richest community of carnivores in North America. Here is an idea you can touch, a vision you can hike into, even as it continues to take shape in our minds and in books such as this.

© Karen Reeves

DOUGLAS H. CHADWICK

Wildlife biologist Douglas Chadwick has traveled the globe reporting on wildlife and conservation, from the Congo headwaters to Siberia to the Great Barrier Reef. He is the critically acclaimed author of *The Fate of the Elephant, A Beast the Color of Winter,* and *True Grizz,* as well as *The Company We Keep: America's Endangered Species* and *Enduring America.* His more than 200 articles have appeared in such publications as *National Geographic,* to which he is a frequent contributor, *Audubon, Defenders of Wildlife,* and *Smithsonian Magazine.* A longtime conservationist, Chadwick spent seven years studying mountain goats and other wildlife in Montana's Bob Marshall Wilderness and Glacier National Park. He lives with his family in northwestern Montana.

Individuals of the Swan Lake Flats gray wolf (Canis lupus) *pack, Greater Yellowstone Ecosystem, Wyoming. Left: Yellowstone gray wolf. Below: Raven* (Corvus corax) *calling*

THE RETURN OF THE WOLVES.

I was snowshoeing up a steep slope in Yellowstone National Park when I spotted it: the footprint of a wolf. Probably a day old, it was the size of my hand with my fingers outstretched. I sat back, stunned: I was in the presence of wolves.

Scanning the surrounding hills, I spotted movement in the distance. Two coyotes on the prowl, noses down, checking here and there for scent marks or the sound of a mouse under the snow. Suddenly the first coyote halted as if it had hit an invisible wall. Both heads came up and turned. Obviously, they had come across the scent of the wolf.

I sat watching, my mind wandering back to my first visits to Yellowstone. At that time, no wolves were left in the park. Although wolf packs had roamed the area when the park was created in 1872, "wolf control" had pretty much wiped out the entire population.

To the surprise of everyone, the absence of wolves had a devastating effect on the ecosystem. If you compare historic photographs of the Hayden or Lamar Valley with the scene today, you will notice a lack of aspen groves and willow bushes. During the absence of top predators such as $\longrightarrow$

55

The Swan Lake Flats wolf pack. Left: Rolling parklands in the Beaverhead National Forest (Centennial National Forest), Idaho. Below: Range-rider Ebby Kunesh in the Beaverhead National Forest. Kunesh works with the Predator Conservation Alliance to minimize encounters between wolves and range cattle.

wolves, ungulates—especially elk—could spend hours leisurely browsing willow and aspen saplings to death. With the return of the wolves, elk are more wary and forced to move around, leaving patches of saplings to grow. With the comeback of willows, another key species is back: the beaver. Willows are the beaver's most important food source. Now the beaver can build dams, providing wetland habitat for ducks, muskrats, moose, and other species.

A howl ripped me out of my thoughts—a deep, long-drawn, melancholic howl. Clearly the howl of a wolf. The coyotes moved back and forth anxiously, their nervousness erupting into a series of barks and their own howls. Another howl of a wolf, answered this time by a second one. Then I spotted them: a pack of eight powerful bodies in thick winter coats. The coyotes quickly absconded.

As the wolves came over the hill into full view, a chill of excitement ran down my spine. What enrichment for the ecosystem of this park, I thought. The return of the wolves.

—F.S.

Lower Falls from Artist View Point at Canyon Village, Yellowstone National Park, Wyoming

REFUGE
Southern Y2Y

Ted Kerasote

*Right: Bighorn sheep (Ovis canadensis) with geyser in the distance,
Yellowstone National Park, Wyoming*

READY TO RUN, WE WAIT ON THE EDGE OF INTERSTATE 90. TO OUR LEFT, cars speed uphill. To our right, trucks roar down from Bozeman Pass, air brakes bawling. Separating the east- and westbound lanes is a thigh-high berm of concrete.

In a momentary break in the traffic, we sprint across the icy concrete, vault the barrier, and make it to the gravel-pocked snow on the far shoulder as a pair of container trucks thunder by, blasting us with twin shocks of air.

"You wonder what the animals think," shouts Lance Craighead, the director of the Craighead Environmental Research Institute, an organization whose scientific studies provide data on how wildlife and humans might live together sustainably. One of the institute's projects is this roadkill study, focusing on 25 miles of Interstate 90 between Bozeman and Livingston, Montana. Fortunately, we haven't met the same fate as the white-tailed deer whose carcasses we've found littering the shoulders of the highway and whose deaths Craighead catalogs three times each week, along with those of other species of wildlife.

We reach a barbed-wire fence—up and over—and then we're down in a culvert, 10 feet (3 meters) high, that animals sometimes use to travel beneath the interstate. Craighead has a camera positioned by the mouth of the culvert, its shutter occasionally tripped when a bear, deer, or mountain lion crosses an infrared beam.

Above us the traffic continues to pound, and Craighead says, "Once you get 20,000 vehicles per day, a highway is impenetrable to wildlife. Bozeman Pass gets that during peak times in the summer. On average it's 10,000 vehicles per day. The purpose of our study is to see how we can mitigate the effects of roads and facilitate wildlife migration between core habitats."

With respect to the southern portion of the Yellowstone to Yukon system, one couldn't find a better place to gauge the challenges faced by this bold conservation initiative. Interstate 90, which runs west to east between Seattle and Boston, not only splits the Bridger and Gallatin mountains, it also cuts the entirety of the Y2Y southern region in half. At the north end of the region, in and around Glacier National Park, there are grizzlies and wolves, mountain lions and elk, moose and deer. At the south end, in and around Yellowstone National Park, there are grizzlies and wolves, mountain lions and elk, moose and deer. In a world prior to the internal combustion engine—say, the world of Lewis and Clark, who passed not far from here—these wildlife populations would have traveled back and forth, through basin and range, over col and divide, looking for food, migrating from summer to winter ranges, and intermingling their genes along the way.

Two centuries later, they are prevented from doing so by barriers such as Interstate 90 and thousands upon thousands of miles of secondary roads as well as urbanized areas such as Gallatin County, with its 74,000 people, 30,000 of whom live in the city of Bozeman itself. Thirty-four percent of these people moved here in the last decade, attracted to this part of the Lower 48 by its wildlife, its renowned wilderness, and its spectacular scenery, qualities that no one person impacts but that our aggregate presence—our subdivisions, our malls, our ski areas, and our airports—erodes day by day.

The Yellowstone to Yukon Conservation Initiative—composed of more than 200 organizations and hundreds of individuals—is trying to integrate this human influx into what remains a relatively intact natural landscape, one that stretches 2,000 miles (3,200 kilometers) along North America's spine from the Wind River Mountains of Wyoming to where the Yukon's Ogilvie Mountains run down to the polar sea. In one state, in one valley, Lance Craighead is doing his bit.

"We've been collecting data for four years," he tells me as he changes the film in the culvert camera, going on to explain that four years is barely enough time to collect a good data set, given the variation in the type and number of animals killed from year to year. "This year alone we've had 115 deer killed as well as 4 elk and 2 black bears, though we had 6 bears killed last year." (The complete list for 2004, when he shows it to me later, is quite a bit longer: 5 badgers, 7 great horned owls, 8 coyotes, 12 porcupines, 22 raccoons, and 39 skunks.)

After Craighead pockets the photo evidence, we sprint back across the highway and continue our drive east toward Livingston, noting the location of road-killed deer along the way. We change film in another camera site before searching the westbound lanes and returning to Craighead's office in Bozeman. There he shows me a Geographic Information Systems map of the area. GIS maps combine different layers of information. This one displays three components: the frequency of roadkill; secure wildlife habitat to the north and south of I-90; and the shortest links between these secure or "core" habitats.

It's in these locations that Craighead hopes the highway department might build overpasses for elk and underpasses for lions and black bears. The former would cost $1 million each, the latter $500,000. But Craighead is quick to point out that these figures aren't all that expensive, seeing that interstate highways themselves cost $1 million per mile to construct and wildlife collisions cost U.S. motorists $1 billion each year in damages. The work would take a few months to complete and once done would serve other species. Wolves and deer, for instance, will use either overpasses or underpasses, according to Craighead, as would many of the other animals that live in this part of the U.S. Northern Rockies: bobcats, weasels, martens, snowshoe hares.

As I stare at the two-dimensional map, with its bright colors, numbers, and graphs, I remember the feeling I had on the highway—watching the traffic and sensing its rumble through my feet. I try to imagine myself as a deer, headlights shining in my eyes,

or a badger, staring at the concrete barriers, insurmountable for me. If the money can be allocated, this hectic and dangerous interstate could have a series of crossings that would allow wildlife to pass in relative peace.

Thoughts of overpasses, underpasses, linkages, and refuges of core habitats linger as I drive the 250 miles home to Jackson Hole, Wyoming—west through the shopping centers of Montana's Gallatin River Valley, south through pastoral ranch lands beneath the Madison Range, their crest of peaks dusted with snow, over Reynolds Pass and down to Idaho's Henry's Fork, where trumpeter swans float idyllically in the still water. I drive along the western boundary of Yellowstone National Park, thick with conifers— its high plateaus remote and already sealed off by winter—before passing beneath the three prominent spires that were once called "the pilot knobs" by the mountain men and are now known as the Grand, the Middle, and the South Tetons. Wending my way through the traffic and increasing number of subdivisions in Teton Valley, Idaho, I'm once again startled at the growth that's taken place in what was a small farming community: a 74 percent increase in population between the 1990 and 2000 censuses. The road climbs over the Tetons and switchbacks down into the 40-mile-long (65-kilometer-long) valley known as Jackson Hole, Wyoming, its southern end busy with cars, housing developments, and an explosion of new retail stores. Atypically for Rocky Mountain valleys, however, this development has been limited to 3 percent of the land base. The other 97 percent of Teton County, Wyoming, is public land—national forest, elk refuge, and national park.

Turning north at the Jackson town square, with its often-photographed elk-antler arches, I head in the direction of these open spaces, soon cresting the long rise that leads into Grand Teton National Park and, twenty minutes later, reaching my house in the small village of Kelly.

Directly on the Gros Ventre River, Kelly once vied for Jackson to be the county seat in the early part of the nineteenth century. It had a sawmill, stores, and a vibrant community of cattle ranchers. In 1925 the Gros Ventre River was dammed by a mudslide 3½ (5½ kilometers) miles upstream from the village. Two years later the dam broke, and a wall of water destroyed Kelly, killed six people, and dashed Kelly's hopes of becoming the valley's commercial and governmental center. Instead, it became a sleepy square mile of old cabins, bordered on its southern side by the National Elk Refuge, on its eastern side by the Gros Ventre Wilderness, and on its western and northern edges by Grand Teton National Park. In fact, the village faces the eastern side of the Teton Range from across the Snake River Plain: a grand and empty prospect of sage, aspen, and cottonwoods, of elk, bison, and pronghorn antelope, of jagged mountains capped by glaciers.

Like most of the people who live in the southern part of Y2Y, most of the residents of Kelly don't make their living directly off the land. We have but a handful of hunting, fishing, and mountain guides, as well as a couple of ranchers, in the village. The rest of us make our livings as National Park Service and Forest Service employees, building contractors, nurses, doctors, physical therapists, filmmakers, writers, modem cowboys, attorneys, teachers, waitpeople, and staffers for nonprofit organizations. I can't think of anyone who wouldn't say he or she wasn't also supported by the big vistas and the pageant of wildlife that passes like a river around the village. In addition, many of us are quite literally supported by elk, antelope, and mule deer, for one of the species, sometimes all three, fill our freezers each year.

It's a refuge—a place of shelter in every sense of the word, one whose broad outlines were created by the intersection of geography and climate. While the prairies were plowed under, the bison and elk slaughtered, and great cities linked by railroads, this high, cold, remote place repelled settlers and was one of the last in the Lower 48 to be homesteaded. In addition, the reason that Teton County, Wyoming, is so free of sprawl—and that just on the other side of the Tetons, Teton County, Idaho, is now so plagued by it—goes back to the region's earliest conservation history. Appropriately, this history is also the Ur-story of Y2Y itself.

It begins in August 1870, when Cornelius Hedges, the U.S. District Attorney for Montana Territory, journeyed into the Yellowstone country along with an exploratory party headed by Henry D. Washburn, the surveyor general of the territory, and Lieutenant Gustavus C. Doane, his military escort. The men marveled at the geysers, bubbling mudpots, and waterfalls, and as autumn began to color the aspens they started their descent from the high country. Making a last campfire, the entire party began to discuss filing claims on the land they had seen so as to make a killing when tourists would flock to the natural wonders. In the official National Park Service rendering of the story, Hedges took exception, saying that Yellowstone "ought to be set apart as a great National Park." Nathaniel P. Langford, another Easterner who had come along on the expedition, became so fired by Hedges's proposal that he lay awake all night thinking about it.

Returning to the East, Langford began to popularize the notion of a national park carved out of the Yellowstone country. He gave lectures and wrote two articles for *Scribner's Monthly*. Although many greeted his tales with skepticism, one person decided to verify his story. This was Ferdinand Vandiveer Hayden, the director of the Geological and Geographical Survey of the Territories. In 1871, on his next exploration, he made sure to swing through the Yellowstone country, taking in tow Thomas Moran, the landscape painter, and William Henry Jackson, one of the innovators of panoramic outdoor photography.

The stunning pictorial record the two men brought back caused even the staid *New York Times* to rethink the era's accepted wisdom that humans should civilize every corner of the globe. "There is something romantic," wrote the newspaper's editors, "in the thought that, in spite of the restless activity of our people, and the almost fabulous rapidity of their increase, vast tracts of national domain yet remain unexplored."

The revisionist history of Yellowstone's founding tells a slightly different story. It points out that the first mention of a national park in the area was made not by Hedges in 1870 but by the then territorial governor of Montana, Thomas Meagher, in 1865. No matter who should get credit for visualizing the world's first national park, the autumn of 1871 saw Congress debating a Yellowstone park bill, introduced by William Clagett, Montana's territorial delegate in Congress. Clagett, however, wasn't interested in setting aside wilderness. Rather, he wanted to protect the area's rare natural curiosities from private speculation. Congress acceded, passing the park bill precisely because it saw

Dr. Lance Craighead at work in Bozeman, Montana, with a map depicting habitat quality of the Yellowstone to Yukon Ecoregion; advertisement for a grizzly zoo at Bozeman Pass along Interstate 90 in Montana

Left: Grizzly bear (Ursus arctos) *dashing through traffic in Yellowstone National Park, Wyoming*

Yellowstone as *useless* for cultivation. In fact, it was and remains so. Without the loss of material gain, the region could therefore be turned into an amusement park and "pleasuring" ground for the people.

Only in the mid-1880s—as the Cinnabar and Clark's Fork Railroad tried to secure a right-of-way through Yellowstone so as to reach mining claims—did the concept of saving nature for nature's sake enter the debate. Congressman William McAdoo of New Jersey opposed the railroad and observed that the park had allowed people to see "the inspiring sights and mysteries of nature that elevate mankind and bring it closer communion with omniscience." Then, employing a line of reasoning still commonly used in the twenty-first century, McAdoo beseeched his fellow representatives to "prefer the beautiful and sublime . . . to heartless mammon and the greed of capital." His eloquence carried the day. The Cinnabar and Clark's Fork right-of-way was defeated 107 to 65 and Yellowstone was preserved unsullied, anchoring the southern terminus of the Y2Y region and setting a worldwide precedent for the preservation of nature.

On the heels of this vote, conservation milestones followed decade by decade: national forests around Yellowstone were first set aside in 1891; Glacier National Park was created in 1910; "primitive areas," the antecedents of wilderness areas, were designated in 1940 along the Continental Divide in Montana; and in 1980 the River of No Return Wilderness, a vast area of unspoiled rivers, peaks, and forests in central Idaho, was signed into existence.

Thus—before the twentieth century had come to a close—the high Northern Rockies of the United States had been preserved from logging, mining, and road-building. In addition, a single valley—Jackson Hole—was left almost entirely pristine by one of the most surreptitious bits of philanthropy in the history of the continent. In 1926 John D. Rockefeller Jr. came down from Yellowstone National Park on his family's summer vacation and visited the Tetons, stunned by the alpine scenery and appalled by the dance hall, stores, cabins, and telephone lines that had been built along the base of the mountains. In secret, he began to buy up ranches on the floor of Jackson Hole, knowing that if he made his plans public they would be quickly scuttled by ranchers and developers. After a tiny Grand Teton National Park was proclaimed in 1929 (one that protected only the high mountain landscape), Rockefeller began attempts to donate the ranch and riparian land he had bought to the federal government. At last, in 1950, his holdings became part of an enlarged Grand Teton National Park.

A significant part of Jackson Hole, Wyoming, was thus moved into the public estate, while Teton Valley, Idaho, just on the other side of the Tetons, remained largely in private hands. One now has unmarred vistas and wildlife, and the other has subdivisions.

A similar story can be told for much of the southern portion of Y2Y: Where land has remained in the private sector, sprawl has metastasized. The Gallatin and Bitterroot valleys, home to Bozeman and Missoula, respectively, are prime examples. Given this pattern, conservationists at the end of the twentieth century began to ask, Absent another new Rockefeller, what mechanisms do we presently have to cluster people and let the wildlife roam free?

One person who addressed this question was Harvey Locke, a fifth-generation Albertan, an attorney, and a conservationist. In 1993 he sat down with some topographic maps around a campfire in the Muskwa-Kechika region of northern British Columbia, struck by how the entire Rocky Mountain chain hung together as a place of similar fauna, flora, and landscapes. Whether he had traveled in Wyoming, Idaho, Montana, Alberta, British Columbia, or the Yukon, he saw the same moose, the same elk, the same grizzlies, the same flowers, and the same trees and glaciers. Reaching for a succinct phrase that would express this consanguinity, he hit upon "Yellowstone to Yukon," or "Y2Y" for short. The moniker also served as a way to conceptualize protecting these far-flung, interrelated ecosystems without excluding humanity.

One strategy that Locke and his many conservation-minded colleagues across the region developed drew on Rockefeller's pioneering effort—buy private land as it comes up for sale and make sure that it's developed in a way that protects its ecological attributes. Never has this been more important than now, as several million acres of ranch lands in the southern Y2Y are about to come onto the market. Their owners, entering their sixties and seventies, are faced with college payments, inheritance taxes, and medical expenses. Many of these ranches are ecological linchpins. Occupying the transition zone between protected public lands and densely populated, historic town centers, they offer winter range to elk, deer, and moose; they contain some of the region's most valuable wetlands, important as nesting and feeding areas for waterfowl and shorebirds; and they also help to create the celebrated visuals of the Northern Rockies: sweeping grasslands and aspen trees rising between valley floor and alpine heights.

To aid communities in their protection of these lands, the Doris Duke Charitable Foundation committed $8.2 million to the Greater Yellowstone Ecosystem in 2001. Various projects have already been completed. Conservation easements have been bought in Montana's Madison and Centennial valleys, and a grassbank has been created outside of Cody, Wyoming, with the aid of The Nature Conservancy. Grassbanks are ranches owned by conservation organizations that make grass available to ranchers in return for some sort of conservation agreement on their properties. In this case, ranchers use TNC's irrigated pastureland while "resting" critical elk and sage grouse habitat on their properties—in other words, keeping it free from grazing. Some of the most extensive wetlands in the Northern Rockies have also been conserved in Idaho's Teton Valley, ensuring that habitat for waterfowl, sandhill cranes, and long-billed curlews will not be paved over. In another partnering effort, ranchers in the Blackfoot River Valley of Montana have worked with a local timber company and TNC to close down logging in the upper valley and secure wildlife habitat protection.

There isn't enough money, however, to buy conservation easements on every crucial ranch property in the Y2Y, nor does every rancher want to put a conservation easement on his or her ground and stay in the livestock business, with its hard physical work and economic uncertainties. Ranches will come up for sale; subdivision and development will occur. In turn, these new houses, stores, and roads will affect the quality of life for people as well as for wildlife. Therefore, when development seems unavoidable, it's crucial that it be undertaken with care if both humans and wildlife are going to find refuge in these landscapes. Unfortunately, many zoning regulations

Historic barn at sunrise in Grand Teton National Park, Wyoming, with the Tetons in the background

promote the opposite: sprawl, congestion, loss of wildlife. Teton Valley, Idaho, is a case in point.

Once an agricultural landscape of potato farms snuggled between the Tetons and the Big Hole Mountains, the valley now has zoning regulations that stipulate a density of one house per 20 acres when agricultural land is subdivided. Consequently, if a farmer owns 100 acres of land, all he can presently do is subdivide his property into five 20-acre lots. This creates a landscape of roads and ranchettes, deters wildlife migration, and provides little sense of community. But if one were to remove the minimum lot size and give him a bonus for clustering development—for instance, a two-house bonus if he clusters five houses on five adjacent, 1-acre lots—one would then see seven houses erected on seven 1-acre lots, with 93 acres left as open space. If clustering is done on a landscape scale, it can build small villages that give people a sense of inhabiting neighborhoods while providing wildlife the habitat it needs. People also get the space they need. Instead of feeling constrained by a checkerboard of fences and No Trespassing signs, they, too, have commons in which to roam.

Of course, some observers point out that people come to the West for privacy. This is not completely accurate. People come for clean air and water, vistas, recreational opportunities, and low crime rates—for what, in every sense of the word, is a refuge from an increasingly fractious and unhealthy world. Not everyone wants to live on 5 to 35 acres, with a long driveway to plow, and no neighbors nearby.

Kelly is a good example of this sort of small community surrounded by large expanses of commons. Most people in Kelly own two town lots—each 50 feet by 150 feet, or one-third of an acre combined. This may sound like a postage stamp to those who remain captivated by the myth of the West. However, as many of us like to point out, our village lies in the middle of a 20-million-acre ranch, the Greater Yellowstone

Ecosystem. Countless town dwellers across the southern Y2Y feel the same about their small towns: Wilderness and wildlife are a stone's throw away, the boundary between the wild and the civilized remaining very porous.

Three characteristics thus seem to distinguish the Y2Y initiative south of the Canadian border today. First, large areas of wildlife habitat have been, and will remain, protected in national parks, wildlife refuges, and forests. Second, a move by conservation organizations to place ranches under conservation easements is helping to preserve existing migration corridors and winter range between protected, high-altitude areas. Third, initiatives to change zoning laws can help create attractive neighborhoods for people while conserving adjacent open space as wildlife habitat. In addition, some in the ranching community are adding a fourth component to the Y2Y mix—running their livestock operations in a way that nurtures wildlife.

Key to this notion is miming the grazing patterns of the historic fauna of the region, bison and elk. These species once created what ecologists call a "disturbance"— nipping off vegetation and spreading seeds in their feces while trampling, turning over, and aerating the ground with their hooves. Local flora has evolved with these disturbances, indeed flourishes because of them. These plant communities can still flourish in the presence of cattle—if, that is, the cows act like wildlife, briefly disturbing plant communities and moving on so the plants can recover.

One of the models for this sort of eco-friendly ranching has been put into practice by Karl Rappold, whose 13,000-acre ranch I visit after a late November storm turns the Rockies white. Founded in 1882, the ranch is located on the Montana Front, a sparsely populated, magical belt of country where the Great Plains meet the upthrust of the Rockies. In fact, the western boundary of the Rappold spread touches the cliffs of the Bob Marshall Wilderness Area.

A man of classic Western features—blue eyes, strong chin, auburn moustache, turquoise bandanna, and black cowboy hat—he drives his pickup toward the mountains and tells me that he understocks his ranch by current standards, running only 300 cow-calf pairs and 100 head of replacement heifers. This has allowed him to achieve a rare détente with the grizzly bears and wolves who live on his ranch and the mountains above it.

The origins of his ranching practices, he explains, go back to the days of the Depression, when his father routinely killed grizzlies who preyed on cattle. In those lean times, there was nothing else to be done; one cow might enable a family to get through the winter.

"But before my father passed away in 1986," Rappold continued, "he told me that the only regret he had was that he'd killed so many grizzly bears, and that they'd almost become extinct. He made me promise that when I took over the ranch, these big bears would always have a home. So I've worked most of my life to make sure that has happened."

His methods are simple though unconventional. He avoids conflicts with grizzlies by breeding his herd earlier in the year than is traditional. The calves are born earlier, so that when they reach summer pasture they're bigger and heavier and not such easy prey for grizzly bears or wolves. He's also worked with the local fish and game department to distribute cattle carcasses along the high perimeter of his ranch. When

hungry grizzlies come out of their dens, they can fill up on the meat of dead cattle rather than moving to the lower ranch to seek out live ones. By the time the grizzlies are done with the carcasses, the grass is green, they're feeding on vegetation (grizzlies are omnivores), and they leave his cattle alone. In fact, the ranch has not lost a cow to a bear since 1959.

This sort of range management has also been profitable. Because Rappold's cattle have ample grass, they go to market at a greater weight than those of ranchers who run more cattle on similar acreage. As he likes to say, "I'm raising the same amount of beef off of 300 head that a lot of guys raise from 600. It's the pounds you put on the truck, not the number of animals, that counts."

Rappold is also outspoken about other ranchers' poor management practices. They stock too many cattle on their range, he tells me, destroying the grass for wildlife and making the cattle themselves weak and undernourished, easy pickings for bears. Ranchers also put cattle into the high country too early, and they don't look for them carefully enough in the fall—he has found his neighbors' cattle grazing happily in the mountains when the neighbors have claimed that their lost stock has been killed by bears.

Stopping alongside some huge grizzly tracks in the snow, which wander directly among the tracks of his cattle, he says, "The bear is somebody easy to blame. But there's been tons of occasions when I'll come up here and see fifty cows grazing on the hillside and there'll be an old bear amongst them, digging anthills up, neither one of them paying attention to the other."

What if he loses a cow to a bear someday? What will he do then? He answers without hesitation. "If a bear should kill one of my cows, it would be an act of Mother Nature, like an electrical storm. I don't feel the bear has to live with us. We have to learn to live with the bear. He was part of this country long before we settled it, and he should remain part of this country. If you don't like living with bears then maybe you ought to be ranching somewhere else."

I think about his words as I drive down the length of the Rockies, from near the Canadian border, back to Jackson Hole: peak and valley, river and forest, town and city. It has not been the easiest place in the world to live. I've seen 54 below. I've had the first-floor windows of my house covered with snow. Some summers, I've watched my grass turn to dust. But there is passion in this weather, and a joy of being out in it. Sometimes the human-caused changes seem overwhelming. South of my house, in the Upper Green River Basin of Wyoming, beneath the spires of the Wind River Mountains—in other words, at the very southernmost extent of Y2Y—3,000 natural gas wells have been drilled and 7,000 more are on the drawing boards as the Bush Administration attempts to win domestic energy security. The attempt can't possibly succeed, since the United States uses 25 percent of the world's oil and gas resources while only 3 percent of those resources underlie its landmass.

It's one more challenge that the Y2Y initiative faces—halting fossil fuel development where it impacts critical wildlife habitat as well as trying to get hydrocarbons out of the ground (where operations are under way) without decimating what's above it. Currently, energy development sits shoulder to shoulder with sprawl as the region's greatest blight and greatest failure to integrate the civilized with the wild.

Rancher Karl Rappold herding cattle along the Rocky Mountain Front, Montana; exploratory test drill site on the Rocky Mountain Front. Left: Wyoming's Shoshone National Forest in summertime

Having come down the familiar, two-lane roads—down the Henry's Fork, over Teton Pass, through Jackson, and north into the park—I turn up the Gros Ventre River and there, just a few miles from the house, spy a large gray wolf. He's walking along a moraine with a jaunty step, the Tetons soaring above him into a cloud-riven sky. He has a black mask, like a malamute's, and he's watching two bull elk, bedded below him. They may very well be his dinner. His mouth opens in a happy dog grin, the wind ruffles his fur, and he settles himself comfortably in the snow with an expression that says, "Ah, life could not be better."

I would have to agree. How many places in the world can you see elk and wolves near your house? Of course, thousands upon thousands of other people would love to live in a place where they could see the same. I was one of them. Twenty years ago I came from Colorado, looking for more space, more snow, and more animals. I never looked back. Therein lies the greatest challenge faced by the Yellowstone to Yukon initiative: how to provide refuge for wildlife while creating homes for the human emigrants who want to inhabit the very same landscape. It's a work in progress, and history will judge how well we do.

TED KERASOTE

Ted Kerasote's work on natural history, wildlife, outdoor recreation, and indigenous people has been published in dozens of periodicals and anthologies, including *Audubon*, *Outside*, *Men's Journal*, *National Geographic Traveler*, *Salon.com*, *The New York Times Book Review*, *The Nature of Nature*, *The Best American Science and Nature Writing*, and *The Best Adventure and Survival Stories*. He is also the author of four books. One of them, *Bloodties: Nature, Culture, and the Hunt*, has been reprinted many times and remains one of the most frequently cited works on the ethics of hunting. His latest book, *Out There: In the Wild in a Wired Age*, won the 2004 National Outdoor Book Award for literature. Kerasote lives in Kelly, Wyoming.

The Tetons reflected in Schwabacher Pond, Grand Teton National Park, Wyoming

Black bear (Ursus americanus) *cub*

Left: Red-shafted northern flicker (Colaptes auratus) *feeding its young*

Preceding pages: Beaver (Castor canadensis) *eating willow leaves and twigs under the last light of evening*

THINKING LIKE AN OWL. It was still dark as I loaded my backpack with camera gear and started wandering through an open, parklike forest. I reached the desired spot and sat down as daylight was just breaking. Silhouettes of trees became visible against the dark blue sky. The cold night temperature created a few patches of fog hovering just above the ground.

Sitting, I awaited the approach of the phantom of the northern forests: the great gray owl, or "the Great Gray Ghost," as it is called. The moon, the silent forest, and the patches of fog set the perfect stage for its appearance. I waited, charged with suspense.

Out of nowhere the owl appeared, floating by me not ten yards away, silent as a ghost. It landed in a conifer tree, its disk-shaped face pointing in my direction. The large yellow eyes fixed on me for a few seconds, but the owl seemed little impressed with my presence. Instead its face registered sounds undetectable to me—a rodent scratching in the dirt, perhaps. I watched the owl until the sun broke over the horizon, filling the landscape with light. Suddenly she took flight into denser forest across a clearing, disappearing from sight.

I had photographs of the owl sitting on a branch. But her flight had been so impressive—how could I get images of that? Something told me the bird would be back. I thought that if she came to the edge of the dense forest, the blinding sun would be in her face. Yet in the

Great gray owl (Strix nebulosa) *and great gray owl chick, Greater Yellowstone Ecosystem, Wyoming*

center of the clearing I spotted an ideal perch. I imagined there was a slim chance the owl would eventually use it.

I lined myself up in the imaginary path the owl might fly—between the forest's edge and the ideal perch. The waiting game began. Two hours passed and nothing happened. Had I been too optimistic? What were the chances of me reading the owl's mind correctly? Just be patient, I told myself. Then, in the middle of my silent dialogue, I noticed a movement at the edge of the forest. Could it be real? I moved over a few paces to be exactly in line with the perch. Doing everything by intuition, I adjusted the camera's exposure and prefocused to a spot where I thought the owl would fill the frame. Then it happened. The owl took off from her forest perch and flew directly in my direction. I caught her in my viewfinder—still blurry—but I could see her coming closer, becoming sharper with every wing beat. Then she came into focus: A magnificent bird, wings five feet across, coming at me with piercing yellow eyes as if I were doomed prey. "Click, click, click." In a split second it was over. The owl flew silently over my head and landed a few yards away on the tree. I was speechless.   —F.S.

The Tetons and Jackson Lake at sunset, Grand Teton National Park, Wyoming

Right: Two bull moose (Alces alces) *fighting*

Pronghorn (Antilocapra americana) *at sunset*

Left: The Lamar River, Yellowstone National Park, Wyoming

Elk (Cervus elaphus) *play-fighting; elk bugling at dusk; Yellowstone National Park, Wyoming*

Left: Grizzly bear (Ursus arctos) *walking through fallen timber*

Scenes from various powwows in the Y2Y region

POWWOW. I am surrounded by dancing bodies, the smell of sweetgrass filling the air. I am caught up in the powerful beat, a rhythm resonating deep inside. It seems as though an ancient drumbeat is echoing back from the mountain walls into this present time. Powerful chanting voices join the drumming, creating a fusion of sound that lasts through the entire night and greets the rising sun.

Native in traditional costume, Crow Indian Reservation, Montana

Powwows have been revived as a way for Native Americans to strengthen their ties to their past. Powwows are a way to recover ancient traditions and recall a philosophy of life that recognizes this Earth as an interconnected web.

Traditional Native American and First Nations beliefs about how we should treat this planet have long been a part of conservation movements in Europe. I am aware that I came to this continent with a romanticized vision of its indigenous peoples. I've come to realize that time did not stand still for them. Decades of exploitation and disrespect have left scars. Yet I've seen how Native groups are regaining their strength and finding their way back to traditional ways, languages, dances, and beliefs, including the belief that we should treat our Mother Earth with respect.

In Montana, for example, the Salish-Kootenay tribes have blocked plans for a major expansion of U.S. Highway 93, demanding that wildlife and environmental needs be taken into consideration. Thanks to the wise elders and the tribal councils, there now are plans for forty-three wildlife crossing structures, and landscape architects are redirecting the highway around sensitive habitat and historic cultural sites.

—F.S.

Pronghorn (Antilocapra americana) herd*; bull elk* (Cervus elaphus) *in sagebrush field*

Left: American badger (Taxidea taxus) *carrying a squirrel to the den*

Castle Geyser backlit by the sun, Yellowstone National Park, Wyoming

Hot spring in Geyser Basin; Clypsedra Geyser; Mammoth Hot Springs; Yellowstone National Park, Wyoming

Left: The Grand Prismatic Spring near Lower Geyser Basin, Yellowstone National Park

Cutthroat trout (Oncorhynchus clarki bouvieri) *in the waters of a shallow river*

Right: Osprey (Pandion haliaetus) *bringing a rainbow trout to the nest*

Evening at Red Rock Lakes National Wildlife Refuge, Montana

Clockwise from top: Trumpeter swan (Cygnus buccinator)*; barn swallow* (Hirundo rustica)*; northern harrier* (Circus cyaneus)*; sandhill cranes* (Grus canadensis)*;
Red Rock Lakes National Wildlife Refuge, Idaho*

Left: Marsh wren (Cistothrous platensis)

RANCHING IN GRIZZLY COUNTRY. Karl Rappold is a rancher on Montana's Rocky Mountain Front. His grandfather homesteaded here in 1882, and Karl will tell you, with a proud spark in his eyes, that with the exception of buffalo, his ranch land is still home to all the wildlife species that were present when Lewis and Clark passed through.

I drove out to Karl's place one September day to talk with him about ranching in grizzly country. Directly ahead of me, a wall of mountains rose out of the flat, grassy plains: the "Front," as they call it around here.

Four cowboys came across the parkland, herding cattle. Four-wheelers haven't replaced horses out here yet. Karl walked over and greeted me with his firm handshake. "Another wonderful day out on the Front," he said, looking around. "Good to see you again!"

I watched as he and his men counted the cattle moving through the gates: 302 total, 4 missing. Were those cows lost to grizzlies? I asked.

Above from far left: The Rocky Mountain Front, Montana; Karl Rappold; Karl Rappold driving cattle through the prairies of the Rocky Mountain Front. Below: Metal sculpture on fencepost at Karl Rappold's Ranch, depicting a practice from a bygone era

"Oh, no," Karl said with a smile. "The last death loss we had to a grizzly was in 1959. Grizzlies graze with the cattle." What's his secret? "Learning to live with them—that's the biggest thing. We manage the farm with grizzlies in mind. That's why we don't send the cattle up into the mountains until they've reached a good size."

When Karl first heard about Y2Y, he thought it was a pipe dream. He has since become instrumental in protecting the Rocky Mountain Front and striking a balance between human endeavors and the needs of wildlife and the environment. The achievements of recent years have convinced him that the goals of Y2Y can become a reality. "Whether you're a rancher, conservationist, environmentalist, or what, everybody has the same goal. I guess it is a dream come true for me, because it means this area will always be protected and will remain like this forever."
                                                                                    —F.S.

Sunrise in the rolling prairie grasslands of the Rocky Mountain Front, Montana

SWIFT FOX PUPS.   Swift foxes, the smaller cousin of the red fox, were reintroduced onto the land of the Blackfeet Indians, in eastern Montana, in 1998. Since the reintroduction project began, more and more of these little creatures are roaming the plains again. I wanted to get a picture of these foxes to tell their story.

I scouted out one of their dens from a far distance but realized I would need several days and a blind to get close enough for good images. The alternative was to try a rather unconventional method. I knew the little pups would be afraid of a human figure approaching and would escape into their den. But on these plains, the foxes are accustomed to having cows around. I had an idea.

Somehow, I convinced my partner, Emil, to play along. We would pretend we were cows. Covered with dark cloths, we would

Swift fox (Vulpes macrotis) *pups near their den in the Rocky Mountain Front, Montana. Below: Long-billed curlew* (Numenius americanus)

slowly "graze" our way toward the fox den, taking long, backward-chewing breaks and conversing in "cow language." Crawling over the prairie, rocking our bodies in a slow, cowlike fashion, we advanced toward the den. "Mooooo," I called to Emil. "Moooo," she answered back.

I am not really sure the foxes thought we were cows. Rather, I had the feeling they were saying to one another, "Look at those idiots crawling across the prairie, pretending to be cows!" Either way, it worked out, and I was able to capture these wonderfully intimate images of the foxes playing together.

—F.S.

Black bear (Ursus americanus) *female with two cubs, Glacier National Park, Montana*

Left: Steep eastern slopes of the Rocky Mountains, Montana

Fall on the Blackfeet Indian Reservation, Montana, with Divide Mountain in the background

Grizzly bear (Ursus arctos) *digging for roots*

THE KING OF THE MOUNTAINS. *I was sitting on a high alpine slope, looking over mountain lakes and ranges. It was a peaceful September day. Flocks of migrating water pipits fluttered by, filling the air with their soft calls, while golden eagles shot through the skies above me, arching in acrobatic grace. It was late afternoon, and slowly the mountain cast a shadow of blue light over me. I had been on that alpine ridge for days, waiting for something to happen. I was watching a large bighorn sheep when I noticed that it had become quite alert. I turned my head, following the direction of its gaze. My eyes met with those of a silver-tipped grizzly.*

It was as if the mountain wall had simply given birth to the grizzly—it appeared that quickly and silently from out of the blue light. In a single instant, it seemed the whole mountain came alive, vibrating with anticipation. In awe I sat there, watching the magnificent creature digging for roots. I knew he was aware of my presence—the wind had long since carried my scent over to him. Slowly the bear came closer, and everything seemed to fall into a hush. Silence filled the place, as if the whole world was holding its breath, watching the king of the mountains enter the stage . . . —F.S.

Jumbo Mountain from Jumbo Pass, Purcell Mountains, British Columbia

THE COURAGE OF HOPE
Central Y2Y

Rick Bass

Right: Glaciers on the west side of Jumbo Pass, British Columbia

In the mid-1990s, when I first heard about the Yellowstone to Yukon concept, I got very excited. I knew there were many parts of this huge canvas of a landscape that I'd never visit, but I liked the idea that a coalition of diverse interests could work to help support an entire region, one that I believe is the spine, soul, heart, and spirit of North America. The Y2Y region is important for the astonishing diversity and vigor of life it contains—the wildness—as well as for the human cultures and communities that continue to build themselves around and into that landscape.

The Y2Y vision is broad and deep. It looks at things as seemingly disparate as salamanders and grizzlies, loons and bog orchids, as well as the intangible and immeasurable necessities that define the region for all of us who are fortunate enough to live here: the sunsets and moonrises, the howling weather, the velvet folds of uncut forest, the sheer and breathtaking slabs of rock and ice.

Y2Y reconnects these things on the ground and in our minds and hearts. To paraphrase the great Wallace Stegner, Y2Y provides a service to all of us—whether we live here or live thousands of miles away—by preserving and celebrating the *idea* of wilderness. It's important to us all, Stegner reminds us, to know that such country exists and is protected—that it will always exist, even if we never set foot into it.

The central section of the Y2Y corridor is the longest leg. Beginning roughly at the U.S.–Canada border, on the Montana, British Columbia, and Alberta boundaries, it proceeds northward through the sometimes-lush, sometimes-icy, forested center of British Columbia, on either side of the spine of the northern Rocky Mountains, up into the immensity of the Muskwa-Kechika country, north of Fort Nelson, and into the northern Y2Y. I am blessed to be able to set foot into this country every day. Living almost literally on the U.S.–Canada border (only 6 miles/10 kilometers) separate me in this lower nation from the upper), I am chagrined when I look south toward the waves of airport expansion, golf courses, ski resorts, and scattershot first- and second-home development. I need and want, and am accustomed to, the reassurance of knowing that wilder country, and lots more of it, begins 6 miles north.

My own little valley, the Yaak, not quite a million acres, lies at the southernmost tip of Canada's largest mountain range, the Purcells, and is the only place where those mountains enter the United States, dwindling to a taper along the Kootenai River. The southern Purcells are compressed from having slept beneath several thousand feet of blue ice during the last period of glaciation, even while most of the other mountain landscapes around them were being carved into dramatic, near-vertical crags of rock and ice.

What is at least as dramatic, to my way of thinking, is the astounding diversity of life that is concentrated in a lower-elevation landscape like the Yaak. There's more moisture and more vegetation, and temperatures are milder; indeed, so productive is this ecosystem that nothing is known to have gone extinct here since the last Ice Age. Particularly valuable to the chain of life in the Yellowstone to Yukon country are these lower-elevation fens and bogs and marshes that support and cleanse so much of the rest of that productive ecosystem and that will be all the more critical to that web of life in a warmer, and warming, world.

One of the things that caught my eye about the Yellowstone to Yukon Initiative initiative was the ground-zero nature of my own existence, residing in the narrowest and hence most vulnerable bottleneck of the Y2Y corridor, at the biological gateway to Canada. It concerns me hugely that in my million acres of the southern Purcells—one of the wildest representations of Y2Y, from a standpoint of biodiversity—there's not one

single acre of permanent protection. I've been laboring for almost twenty years now to help correct this oversight. Soon after Y2Y was conceived, I sent a note to Harvey Locke, an Alberta conservationist and one of the founders of Y2Y, letting him know that with the Yaak at the rough midpoint between Yellowstone and the Yukon, as well as in that critical, narrowest bottleneck, I would be thinking of the venture as "Y3Y"—Yellowstone to Yaak to Yukon.

Spurred by the Y2Y vision, a couple of autumns ago I traveled to Waterton-Glacier International Peace Park, another of the Y2Y hot spots, right on the U.S.–Canada border, in British Columbia and Alberta. I went up and over rugged Crowsnest Pass—yet another migratory bottleneck where wildlife habitat, highway, and steep cliffs intersect, and where conservation corridors must be established—and down into the soft sweet country along the Rocky Mountain Front. There, dotted with hayfields and power-generating windmills, serene prairie rolls up into the near-vertical crashing of frozen stone—rocks that about 200 million years ago rested over the Yaak region before being lifted up and thrust eastward. In Waterton, where there are plans to expand the Peace Park to include the headwaters of the North Fork of the Flathead River, I backpacked with Locke, Steve Thompson of the National Parks Conservation Association, and Adam Witkowski of Road-Rip, an organization that specializes in restoring watersheds damaged by too much roadbuilding, logging, mining, and grazing. (Recently, a new threat appeared from out of nowhere: The Canadian government has permitted major coalbed methane development just across the border, without even notifying the United States.)

On my trip into Waterton, as always happens in such big country, time fell away, so that I lost track of the hours and then, wonderfully, the days. This is one of the great gifts of the Y2Y country, and while we all sense a moral duty to safekeep the genetic and biological charge of life intact within these spectacular landscapes, it is not ignoble to remember, from time to time, what's also in it for us: the restoration and rejuvenation that our own spirits can receive from even a brief time spent in such splendor.

We saw evidence of nature's force written in the geology of the region by the massive yet sophisticated hands of time, and yet we saw life as well. A harlequin duck resting below the rapids. A black bear mother sending her cubs up an aspen tree to protect them from our ponderous approach. The improbable courage—or was it nonchalance?—with which mountain goats passed over the sheer cliffs above the proposed park expansion. And taking our lunch high on a windy peak, staring down into the unprotected Wigwam drainage—staring into the future, we hoped, of an area soon to be protected—we heard a voice singing, there in the wilderness, as a falcon hovered over us, watching us watch the country. Angels, or mountain spirits, we wondered? No, it was just a yodeler, a park ranger in shorts and knee socks on her

Left: Grizzly bear (Ursus arctos) *at edge of larch forest, Assiniboine Provincial Park, British Columbia*

day off, wind- and sun-burnished, exalting in the mountains' glory, and a tad surprised to find us there, tucked in behind the rocks, out of the wind's howling way. When we announced ourselves, and asked her how she felt about the proposed park expansion, she said she thought it was a wonderful plan, that we needed all the wilderness we could find, these days. And though she was polite enough not to say it, I couldn't help wondering whether she wouldn't have preferred, that day, to broaden the park beyond even the proposed expansion, in order to have her yodeling peak to herself, if only for that afternoon.

The Y2Y coalition is using scientists—geneticists, conservation biologists, hydrologists, wildlife scientists, and others—to help guide management proposals and to craft a plan connecting wildlands that offers our best hope of preserving a way of life that includes human communities living at the edge of a great and sometimes vast wildness. Ultimately, this chain of wildness will be only as strong as its weakest link. Again, my thoughts are drawn back to the critical low-elevation "Yaak-to-Yahk" bottleneck (between my own Yaak Valley and the east Kootenay town of Yahk in British Columbia) and to places like Crowsnest Pass—and despite our best plans, the animals do not always, in the peregrinations necessary to their survival, stay within those corridors we've drawn. The thing that many of them need most—particularly the spectacular megafauna that so define the region—wolverine, grizzly, lynx, wolf, caribou, mountain goat, bighorn sheep, lion, elk—is big country, and lots of it.

And where they no longer have this—where their lives and cultures are disrupted by the habitual and increasing intersection with our own—we *are* trying, in the best way we know how. There are places where we cannot turn back the hands of time even if we wanted to; so instead, engineers are laboring to create safe passageways, or at least avenues of reduced mortality, under and over the main arterials of our disruption.

Highway overpasses for large mammals, as well as underpasses for smaller creatures, are springing up throughout the New West, looking in part like outdoor art projects, to the point where they are not only a source of increased civic pride, as well as an extra layer (if thin) of protection against costly vehicle-animal collisions, but also a constant reminder that out there on the larger, farther, wilder landscape, there still reside the wild creatures that still, even in the twenty-first century, help give our lives meaning and shape, enriching our days and our imagination.

Such structures are no substitute for the wild, of course. I worry that as we lose more and more of our wild country, there are those among us who one day won't even know the nature and magnitude, the wonder, of what we've lost. I worry that one day soon we will confuse scenery with spirit, recreation with prayer. That we will find peace in the sylvan green of an artificially nourished golf course, and pride of craft in the construction of a 52,000-bed international ski lodge perched precariously atop a sliding, slipping, retreating film of dirty, vanishing ice in these last days of a cooler world.

I worry that we will one day soon inhabit a world where everything is for sale,

Top and middle: Bull elk (Cervus elaphus) *and black bear* (Ursus americanus) *crossing highways in British Columbia. Bottom: A wildlife overpass on the Trans-Canada Highway in Banff National Park, Alberta*

Right: Aerial of the Trans-Canada Highway and wildlife overpass in Banff National Park

and where the concept of leaving a piece of wild country alone and intact, free to pulse and respire under its own rhythms, will seem utterly alien to us.

And when the young and gifted photographer Florian Schulz invited me up farther into southern Canada, to visit one of his favorite places with him, a place called Jumbo Mountain, 150 or so miles (240 kilometers) north of the U.S.–Canada border, on British Columbia's west side of the Continental Divide, I worried then, too. To an experienced fretter such as myself, even the name seemed foreboding: *Jumbo.* Something big and therefore rare, in a world where it seems all large things are forced toward diminution.

I follow Florian's directions northward, along the cleavage between the East and West Kootenays, until I reach the resort town of Invermere, where I turn west and head up farther into the mountains. After a while I pass the ski resort of Panorama, and the road narrows to rocks and gravel. Florian's directions say to continue on this road until it ends.

Stones thunk and clatter against the undercarriage of my car, yellow cottonwood leaves swirl in the autumn winds, and the tops of the mountains on either side of the narrow canyon gleam with the season's first snow. The sky is blue, even as the canyon is dark and cold. Why is there even a road here in the first place?

Florian is waiting for me at the trailhead, where, after introductions, we load our packs and start up the trail toward the high ridge far above, where Florian and his partner, Emil, have been staying in a stone hut for a few days and where on this day she has chosen to relax and wait for us. As we hike higher and higher, passing through old spruce forests, more of the Jumbo Valley becomes visible through the trees, like the glimpses of light seen through the stained glass of a church window. In the high cirque of the basin, we spy a couple of old clearcuts, tiny and ridiculous—faint scrapings on nearly sheer slopes, where the soil has since washed away to reveal bare gray rock. I explain to Florian that this is the way it was done back in the United States, too; how industry and renegade government land-management agencies would conspire to punch a network of roads, using taxpayer money, as far into the mountains as they dared, for any bogus reason. In the case before us, a 30-mile (48-kilometer) road, costing $5 million, provided access to a few loads of stunted timber—doing priceless damage to pristine wildlife habitat in the process, and leaving behind an environmental liability that the taxpayers would then have to either assume or ignore.

The higher we climb, the more beautiful the valley below us becomes, as do the high shelves and basins into which we are climbing. We talk some about the book project, and Florian cautions me that he thinks it's important to stay positive in our message—to improve people's vision of this area—to make them gasp at the beauty herein, a beauty they previously might not have known existed.

And it's here, all around us; he's right. And he's right, I know, to not want to jump right in with lamentations, the long list of threats that seem to attend every magnificent landscape and every stunning animal. To instead let the first-time voyagers, the new recruits and acolytes to the beauty of the region, come along at their own pace; to maybe

fall in love first, and *then* mature to action. It was that way for all of us; why should we, in our desperate haste now, forget the necessity that love must come first?

And yet: For places like Jumbo, such time may not exist. Even now, a ski-town permit has been issued, over widespread local as well as international opposition, and with no scientific or engineering studies. An Italian investor has received permission to build an entire village on top of the Jumbo Glacier, in the heart of the southern Purcells. Such construction would devastate the Jumbo area immediately, from a wilderness perspective, but it would also act as a catalyst for coming extinctions, causing the narrowed taper of all the rest of the southern Purcells, including my home a few hundred miles south, to break away from the main chain of wildness, like the floe of a calving iceberg breaking into the sea.

We're nearing the ridge, sweating hard, even in the late-day crispness of September rolling over into October. The forests are burning with the orange-gold of tamarack; just beyond us, the alpine country is stippled with ice and snow, and even with a few brave wildflowers, whose entire season of life, of blossom and pollination, is compressed into a few weeks. Wildflowers cling to an inch or two of soil that has been 10,000 years in the making, and for which late September and the first few days of October—most other plants' and most other creatures' autumn—is spring, summer, and autumn all rolled into one: the burst, the rush, of life, and then quick senescence, followed by the deepest and coldest of sleeps.

Each step on the trail takes us higher into this country. We are enveloped by beauty now, and by the most elegant, fitting, and hard-gotten kind of grace—and once more, Florian can tell my thoughts, for he says, "First, we have to make them love it."

We gain the ridge, where new valleys fall away on all sides of us, each one as beautiful as the next, and waiting to be explored—waiting as if they had been formed for us 10,000 years ago, in order that we might know and love and explore them, though on their own terms. We're sweat-drenched, quad-burning, and exultant.

When we finally reach the stone hut, Emil is sunning on the porch, and it feels as if we have stepped back in time a hundred years. How rare—and valuable—is such an experience these days?

We talk about Jumbo for a while and ponder aloud about southern Canada in general, fretting over the chicken-and-egg question: *Can Montana survive if the southern Purcells and Kootenays fall?* and, conversely, *Can the southern Purcells and Kootenays survive if Montana falls?*—and then the day is vanishing.

Florian's anxious to rush back up to a certain peak he's been working for days, learning the arc of the sun's path and its effects upon the basin and ridges below—the way it ignites, near day's last gasp, the orange candletips of those larch forests below and bathes the glacier in a strange red-pink. So he and Emil gather up their 100 pounds or more of equipment and hurry off, here at what feels like the top of the world, and I

take a trail in the other direction, delighted by what I consider to be one of the feelings of ultimate richness: always having new country to explore.

I crest a pass in the firelight sepia of alpenglow and start laughing with pleasure, joy, awe, wonder. Always, in wild country, it is this way: You feel relieved, upon entering such territory, whether it is new to you or much familiar. You feel born again: Here lies yet another world, grander than so many others.

There's a fierce wind up on the ridge. I sit behind an upturned slab of mountain to watch the end of day, to witness that orange blush of ancient alpine larches below. Their canopy, floating far below me, seems a lake of cooling, molten orange. I sit there for a long time. The setting sun sends red sundials into the violet sky, and brilliant stars appear. My hands are numb; it feels like January, not September. In the valley behind me, the crevasses seem to grow and widen, darkening in the twilight. Call it whatever you want—God, Allah, Pan—but how could someone *not* worship the force as well as the design and spirit that made these mountains and that keeps them among us, abiding, even now?

That evening, as we dine by candlelight in the hut, Florian hits the high points again. He's relentless at staying on message and indefatigable in his hopefulness. "We need to improve our vision," he says, "we need to be positive." There's still room for sustainable development in the region, he says, but the connectivity between the wildest places must be protected or enhanced, and there must be more protected areas. We can't afford any more conservation "black holes," such as the Yaak. The entire living organism of the wild Northern Rockies—the gold standard of wildness on the North American continent—is at stake.

"Y2Y had always been in me," Florian says, remembering what it was like when he first heard of the project. He saved his money, bought his equipment, and came over to this continent from Germany to witness what had been only a dream and to pursue that dream.

It had been much the same for Emil. She first heard about Y2Y in Mexico City, from Florian. She looked at some of his photos and decided that she had to see the country, too, even though up to that time she'd never been out of Mexico City. She had never dreamed, she says, that such a world existed. She got on a bus and journeyed north 3,000 miles (4,800 kilometers) to see it, evincing, like Florian, another kind of courage—the courage of hope.

It's beautiful, this cloudless, starry night, up on Jumbo: up on the top of the world. If one doesn't think of the future, it's absolutely perfect, with the mountain's enthralling beauty matched exquisitely by its once-upon-a-time promise of geological endurance.

Numerous small and beautiful rock-and-ice parks stipple the landscape north of Jumbo—the fantastic Bugaboo Provincial Park, and the extension of the forested Selkirk Range. Even amid such amazing and glaciated scenery, this region, like every wild region, needs an icon, a beacon of hope and wildness, and in the central Y2Y, only another 60 or so miles (100 kilometers) east of Jumbo, Mount Assiniboine is that beacon. Mountain goats climb Assiniboine's cliffs (as do some humans). Historically, grizzlies have always been drawn to the lush high basins flanking and surrounding it, and they still are.

A big mountain radiates a kind of magic, a special force and an aura, and Assiniboine is that kind of mountain. Big country radiates that same kind of force and aura, and the Rockies of southern Canada—despite the fragmentation of the past century—are still, in many places, that kind of country.

Assiniboine's beauty is not "merely" surficial, the physical elegance of an ice sculpture crafted by the frigid claws of the ice of the ages. Wildness and ecological health surround Assiniboine. This is what the best and most wisely protected areas do: They serve as cornerstone or foundation of all the values we hope to preserve, while providing connectivity between other areas, like the links in a chain. And while it is true that the weak link in a chain determines the ultimate low-end strength of that chain, it is also true that the ultimate capacities of strength and beauty and function are measured by the strongest link; again, to the human eye, Assiniboine is as strong and as beautiful as wild country gets.

Biggest of the big in the central Y2Y, of course, is the internationally acclaimed Jasper-Banff area: the pride of Canada, as Yellowstone is the pride of the United States. Banff was Canada's first national park, established in 1885. If we had had a crystal ball back then and had known all that was coming in the next 120 years, we probably would have wanted to make it much larger, widening its bottlenecks and stretching it all the way up through the Jasper country and William Switzer Provincial Park, and into the Muskwa-Kechika, pulling in more of the lower elevations and wetlands across which the safe passage of wildlife was, back then, taken for granted.

Banff and Jasper are the prototypical big-and-beautiful parks, comparable in many ways to the Greater Yellowstone Ecosystem of the southern Y2Y. They draw in millions of visitors from all over the world to gaze not just at unspoiled nature, but at such vast quantities of it, and to hope for a glimpse of wolves, grizzlies, mountain goats, bighorn sheep, and all the other wildlife that is no longer so abundant (or perhaps not even present) elsewhere in the world.

Banff, with its spectacular visual allure, as well as its size—2,564 square miles (6,641 square kilometers)—which allows it to support so many outlying communities, has, since its creation, been cut into two pieces by a four-lane highway. Some wildlife overpasses have been created—certainly, not enough—and even with the overpasses,

One of the ten coal mines operated by Elk Valley Coal, just south of Crowsnest Pass, British Columbia; mining truck used in the Elk Valley coal mines

Left: Castle Crown Wilderness, Alberta, an area threatened by oil and gas exploration

Grizzly bear (Ursus arctos), *Jumbo Pass, British Columbia; Jumbo Mountain; Jumbo Glacier. Right: Pincher Creek gas plant just north of Waterton Lakes National Park, Alberta*

there is still a drastic diminution of connectivity, with hugely greater costs for wildlife attempting such migrations; and now another major highway (Highway 3) is being expanded. The overpasses and underpasses can reduce the rate of loss, but regardless of how many are implemented, every new road, and every new car passing through, brings a cost to the entire ecosystem. If we are going to preserve even the status quo of the thing we profess to love and be inspired by, we must at least match our zeal for construction and development with the same zeal for celebration and protection, and we must reconnect these increasingly isolated islands of beauty and ecological sanity.

Despite its size, the Banff-Jasper region is also an ambivalent reminder that preservation of natural beauty can serve a local or regional economy far better than the extraction of its resources—and yet living proof, too, that with that preservation comes a serious responsibility to prevent the protection itself from harming the resource. "Industrial tourism," the late Edward Abbey called it, or "industrial wreckreation," as a new generation of activists call it: the danger of loving a place to death.

In the absence of the truly vast regions of wild country—places like the Ireland-sized Muskwa-Kechika region of the northern Y2Y—it is the establishment of a greater series of parks and protected lands that will carry us into the future; and the degree of connectivity between these islands—particularly as ecological change begins to proceed rapidly, in a warming world—will determine the degree of success we achieve in this preservation of wildness. Now, more than ever—not just for reasons of social sanity and healthy outdoor recreation, but for ecological stability—the stressed and changing natural world needs some extra territory within which to work its magic, needs desperately some buffer areas in which to make its supple and elegant transition.

Any list of the incredible—and incredibly wild—places in the central Y2Y will be only a partial one, at best, and any recitation of the challenges involved in protecting and managing that wildness would run the risk of sounding like quite a litany of woe indeed. *Keep it positive*, we are reminded, even while working ceaselessly to make such visions as Y2Y a reality: protecting the Columbia Wetlands, Pincher Creek country along the spectacular and sheer Rocky Mountain Front, the Selkirks and their high-elevation populations of woodland caribou, the lush Elk Valley (with its coal mines and golf courses), and so many more.

For the Y2Y vision as a whole to succeed, this middle link between the southern and northern Y2Y is absolutely vital; lose it, and we lose also the leading edges at either end. It is in many ways the foundation of the entire dream.

"There are no hopeless cases," writes conservation biologist Dr. Michael Soulé, "only people without hope, and expensive cases. That is, given the resources, even a handful of individuals can constitute the basis of a successful effort to salvage a population or species." He is speaking of endangered species' populations, but it occurs to me that he could also be addressing the visionaries, dreamers, and activists of the Y2Y Initiative.

And one of the greatest things about Y2Y is that upon closer examination, that which seems like a fantastic dream is *not* a dream, but a reality; it still exists, even if tenuously, into this new century. The pictures in this book are real, the animals are real, the places are real, as are the spaces between them.

Beyond Y2Y's advocacy and outreach about the importance of wild places, this is another of the great values of the Initiative: the way it focuses the mind on the magnitude of the problem and yet upon the viability of the solution.

What thrills me, as a lover of wild places, is that there are people of all ages working together toward a vision of greatness: people with the energy of a Florian Schulz, aspiring toward what Wallace Stegner called "a society to match our scenery."

How much of the work is altruistic—performed for the benefit of future generations we will never see or know—and how much of it is more immediate and self-focused, given our own passionate love for this vast landscape, is hard to say and, in the end, perhaps irrelevant.

What is not irrelevant is whether we succeed or fail. The first step, as Florian would remind us all, is to open our hearts and leap: to dare to love without reservation, and then to believe.

© Nicole Blaisdell

RICK BASS

Rick Bass is the author of twenty-one books of fiction and nonfiction, including *The Ninemile Wolves, The Roadless Yaak: Reflections and Observations About One of Our Last Wilderness Areas,* and most recently a novel, *The Diezmo*. His stories have been awarded the Pushcart Prize and the O. Henry Award and have been collected in *The Best American Short Stories*. Bass is a board member of the Yaak Valley Forest Council, Round River Conservation Studies, Cabinet Resource Group, and Montana Wilderness Association. For nearly twenty years he has been active in the attempts to help protect the last roadless lands of the Yaak Valley—the lowest elevation, wettest habitat, and narrowest bottleneck of the Y2Y section of the United States. Known as Montana's only rainforest, the Yaak still doesn't have a single acre of designated wilderness.

Bull moose (Alces alces) *with velvet on its rack*

Left: Bow Lake and Crowfoot Glacier, Alberta

Hiker in Johnston Canyon, Banff National Park, Alberta

Right: Kokanee salmon (Oncorhynchus nerka) *in the Kootenay River, British Columbia*

Bull elk (Cervus elaphus) *bugling*

Left: Fall in the Castle Crown Wilderness, Alberta

Aspen trees (Populus tremuloides) *in the Bighorn Wilderness, Alberta*

Loons (Gavia immer) *in the Bighorn Wilderness, Alberta*

FLY-FISHING. Imagine a place where you cast your line over crystal water. Your eyes follow the path of the fly back and forth across the river in a constant rhythm, back and forth, back and forth. Then suddenly you catch a movement from the corner of your eye. You turn quickly and see a bull elk emerging out of the thicket to get a drink of fresh water.

—F.S.

130

Bull elk (Cervus elaphus)

Left: Fishing in Alberta, the Three Sisters in the background

Mother moose (Alces alces) *and calf at Bowron Lakes, British Columbia*

Right: Black bear (Ursus americanus) *wandering shore in Bowron Lakes area*

Angel Glacier on Mount Edith Cavell, Jasper National Park, Alberta

Left: Mount Edith Cavell reflected in Cavell Lake

North American river otters (Lutra canadensis)

RIVER OTTERS AT PLAY.   I came across a very strange-looking track in the snow while cross-country skiing. It was a long and narrow indentation, as though someone had dragged something across the ice. But this couldn't be possible because no footprints were visible alongside the drag mark. Then it hit me. A river otter! River otters skitter across the surface of the snow on their smooth fur. I followed the track to an opening in the ice, where I discovered a family of otters.

For several days I watched and photographed the river otters. They are the most playful and carefree creatures I have ever seen. (And the mothers among the most patient.) The otters would climb out of the water onto the ice, where the young would bite their mother's tail, chase each other, and roll around in the snow. All tangled in a ball, they would bite each other's fur and tumble back into the freezing water. Back to fishing, they would disappear for a few moments between the cracks of the ice, until they emerged once again on another floe farther downstream. It was a sheer joy to watch them!

—F.S.

Mount Assiniboine in late fall, Assiniboine Provincial Park, British Columbia

Right: Mount Engadine and a moose (Alces alces) family at Spray Valley Provincial Park, Alberta

American pika (Ochotona princeps)

Left: Opabin Valley and Mount Shäffer at the Lake O' Hara area, Yoho National Park, British Columbia

Mountain goat (Oreamnos americanus)

Right: Mountains along the Icefield Parkway in Jasper National Park, Alberta

Howser Peak, Bugaboo Provincial Park, British Columbia

Columbia Mountains, looking south from Abbot Ridge, Glacier National Park, British Columbia

Bison (Bison bison) *on a foggy morning in the Muskwa-Kechika Management Area, British Columbia*

Left: Helmcken Falls, Wells Gray Provincial Park, British Columbia

The Wilder Side of a Wild Walk
Northern Y2Y

Karsten Heuer

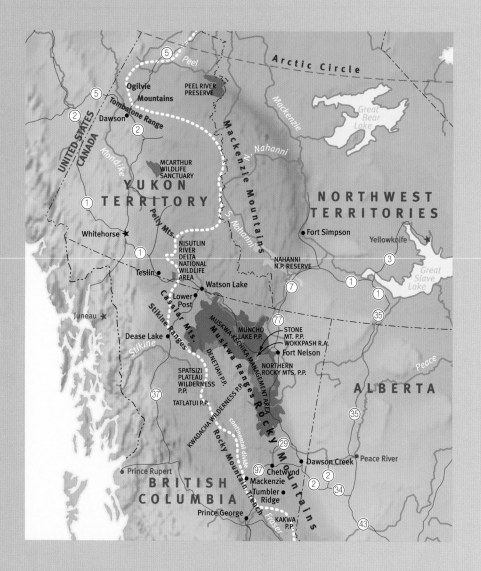

Right: Sunrise at Tochodi Lakes, Muskwa-Kechika Management Area, British Columbia

IF I'D DEFINED THE GEOGRAPHY OF MY EXPECTATIONS BEFORE STARTING THE hike from Yellowstone to the Yukon, it would have conformed nicely with the boundary between the central and northern reaches of the Y2Y region. South of Jasper, Alberta is a place of busy highways, spreading subdivisions, burgeoning ranchettes, and overcrowded parks; north is a sparsely populated and inaccessible land where wildlife still flourishes. Eighteen months and 2,200 miles (3,500 kilometers) later, I would realize such expectations were only partly right.

Pull out a road map of the Y2Y region and you'll see what shaped and colored my thinking. To the south, protected areas like Yellowstone, Montana's Gates of the Mountains Wilderness, and the Waterton-Glacier International Peace Park appear as islands in a grid of red lines and black dots. But to the north, lesser-known parks like the Willmore Wilderness, the Cariboo Mountains, the Tombstones, the Muskwa-Kechika Management Area, the Spatsizi Plateau, and Nahanni National Park still float in a matrix of green. Trace a 400-mile-wide (600-kilometer-wide) swath through that greenness, run it to the Arctic Circle, and the scale of the northern reach of Y2Y begins to hit home: half of northern British Columbia, a sixth of the Northwest Territories, two-thirds of the Yukon, and the vast majority of undeveloped watersheds left in the Rocky, Cassiar, and Mackenzie mountains. Stone, bighorn, and Dall sheep graze in the eastern-front ranges of this huge area, wolverines wander through the buckling interior mountains, and, to the west, grizzly bears feed on salmon a mere 200 miles (300 kilometers) from the rugged Pacific Coast. It is a land of few towns (fewer than twenty) and few paved highways (two). A land where wildlife trails outnumber roads 10 million to one.

FROM BANFF TO Y2Y

When I first heard of the audacious Y2Y vision in 1995, I was too involved with a fight for local wildlife corridors to take it seriously (a fight that, despite five years of carefully compiled research, we lost). Houses and golf courses were approved from one side of Alberta's Bow Valley where I lived to the other, and in the course of half a decade the best low-elevation route for wildlife in and out of Banff National Park was blocked by such development. Wintering moose could no longer get to their summer range, denning bears couldn't reach their favorite berry patches, and potential prey became unavailable to a pack of hungry wolves.

As a practicing wildlife biologist, I understood that the impacts of such poorly planned development were more than local. Radio-collared wolves had moved through the area on their way to Montana, Idaho, and northern British Columbia, as had lynx, cougars—even elk—that had ventured beyond the borders of Banff Park. The routes getting blocked in Alberta's Bow Valley were part of a regional network used by wildlife to find food, mates, and new territories, and to escape fire, flood, and disease. Yet land developers and planners were entrenched in old patterns, looking no farther than their own jurisdictions. Frustrated with such parochial thinking, I soon found myself reconsidering what I'd initially dismissed as too bold a vision. If conserving regional wildlife was the goal, I realized, then nothing less than a broad-scale vision like Y2Y would suffice.

But was it possible? Did the corridors at the heart of a reserve network that spanned half a million square miles even exist? I called Canadian and U.S. colleagues and spent

Caribou (Rangifer tarandus) *walking along a river. Right: Hiker crossing a river in the Muskwa-Kechika Mangement Area, British Columbia*

time in the local university library, but soon realized that what I sought couldn't be found on the phone or in reports or books. The land held the answers to my questions, and to hear and see them I would have to move like a wolf or a grizzly bear, traveling from one Y to the other, step by step and on the ground.

LOOKING FOR GRIZZ

If the purpose of the hike was to gauge the plausibility of Y2Y, I needed a measure, and what I settled on as I walked out of Yellowstone was the presence or absence of the wilderness-dependent grizzly bear. Where I saw signs of recent activity, I assumed the cores and corridors of Y2Y were still possible; where I didn't, I presumed they'd been lost. Having worked on numerous projects studying the reclusive animals, I knew what to look for: tracks, rub trees, digs, and scat. If I was lucky, I might even glimpse the odd animal from afar.

A snow avalanche, the end of a two-year relationship with my girlfriend and hiking partner, a couple of near-misses with lightning, and a few bear encounters all muddled the pattern, but by the time I'd covered 1,200 miles (1,900 kilometers) and reached Jasper, Alberta, in the fall of 1998, I figured I had a trend. Without exception,

the islands of grizzly bear habitat were growing as I moved north. It took one month to traverse the Waterton-Glacier protected-area complex and two months to walk the conglomerate of protected areas around Banff and Jasper, with smaller gaps between (two weeks of cow pies, four-wheel-drive trails, and subdivisions north of Yellowstone; four days of mines, cottages, and clearcuts in British Columbia's Crowsnest Pass). If all I'd heard about points north was true, then there would be little if any development from there on.

Or so I thought.

GUIDED BY WOLVERINE

The grizzlies were still hibernating when I continued north on skis after a three-month break in Jasper, and I left town with a new indicator by which to measure wildness, as well as a new companion. Both were strong, beautiful, and tenacious lovers of big, open spaces. One was the wolverine; the other was my future wife.

We weren't more than a few days into what promised to be the tougher half of a tough trip before Leanne and I got turned around. Physically, not figuratively, and not once but twice. Backing out of the dead-end canyon took hours of precious effort, and so did retreating from a false pass, but after doing so we noticed what we'd missed in our initial hurry: two-by-two tracks that avoided the hidden obstructions and went north in an aesthetic, graceful line. Somewhere in the trailless outback between Mount Robson Provincial Park and the Willmore Wilderness, we traded map and compass for the wisdom of wolverine.

For the next twenty-eight days, so long as we stayed close to the wolverine tracks crisscrossing that country, we found a way around frozen waterfalls, through the deadfall of old forest fires, and across thinly iced rivers. When we didn't, there were problems: another near-miss with an avalanche; a deadly fall stopped short by a snow shelf; and a flounder through thick bush that transformed an hourlong shortcut into a two-day ordeal. By the time we reached the town of Tumbler Ridge in the eastern foothills of British Columbia's Northern Rockies four weeks later, we were exhausted and humbled, but deeply content. The animals had taught us something about moving—something about flow—and we struggled not to lose it as the first signs of humanity crept in.

LOSING SIGHT OF THE VISION

The path into Tumbler Ridge had been laced with coal mines, and it was clearcuts, gas wells, oil rigs, and flare stacks that lined the trail out. The snow was melting, bears were coming out of their dens, but there were no grizzlies along the Murray, Peace, or Halfway rivers. Bulldozers, logging trucks, and other heavy equipment were all that moved for the next seven days, and we wound through all of it in a surprised state of shock.

"Last time I saw a grizzly around here was years ago," said Bruce Simpson, a rancher we met in the Halfway River Valley. "Back when we were still at the end of the road."

Simpson's ranch wasn't anywhere near the end of the road any more. In the last 6 miles (10 kilometers) Leanne and I had passed five new road junctions, each bristling with signs pointing to new oil and gas wells. And unlike Simpson's old neighbors, the people driving the out-of-province pickups didn't even slow down as they passed, let alone wave.

"Goin' to check their dials so they can call the numbers in to head office," said Simpson once the dust had cleared. "Makin' sure enough of the black gold is still flowing south."

Like the Amazon, the Congo, and other far-flung places in the world, Bruce Simpson's once-quiet homestead was being impacted by globalization. Trees, oil, gas, and minerals that were once too remote to extract were suddenly profitable in the age of mass transportation, labor-saving technologies, and dwindling world supply—a trend that has by no means been limited to the Peace and Halfway river valleys of Y2Y. The Yukon's first industrial-sized lumber mill started in the southeast corner of the territory in the late 1990s; plans for new mines bordering Nahanni National Park are in the latter stages of development; and with rumors of a Mackenzie Valley pipeline flying, Albertan and Texas-based companies are racing to find oil and gas in the Peel, Porcupine, and other Arctic watersheds. Contrary to popular belief, the need to establish connections for wildlife is as urgent in the north as it is in the south.

What differs, of course, is the dynamic that threatens them. Unlike the southern end of Y2Y, where the problems are often rooted in too many people loving a place to death (overcrowding of parks, subdivision of open ranchlands into retirement homes and executive retreats), an increasing number of wild areas in the north are in trouble because too few people love them enough. Scattered over vast distances, the sparse human population holds few activists, few recreational interests, and few organized citizen groups to champion a conservation cause. Those that do are far apart, rendering the area ripe for multinational corporations to move in. Resources are still plentiful, and opposition to how, when, and where these resources are taken hardly exists.

I watched as another pair of pickups rumbled past Simpson's house, and then I slowly scanned his yard. Fences were down, the old barn was half toppled over, but beside the weed-covered and rusted farm machinery sat a well-used bulldozer and a number of newer pieces of heavy equipment.

"Things got happening so fast it was either join in or lose out," said Simpson as he followed my eyes. "Cattle prices went through the floor, cost of farming through the roof, and I wasn't left much choice." Having hit hard times, Simpson now spent most of his days pushing more seismic line and more roads deeper into the mountains.

I wanted to tell him about other ranchers I'd met farther south, ones who'd worked with conservation groups to battle the cash squeeze, but the poverty I witnessed kept me quiet. It was an old derelict mobile home we stood beside, and out its door came a long procession of sons, daughters, daughters-in-law, and grandchildren while we talked. Despite the tax incentives, and despite the benefits for wildlife, the kind of easements that curbed suburban sprawl farther south couldn't do much for a man caught between industrial development and how to feed his family their next meal.

TOWARD A HIGHER ORDER

Given the threats, pressures, and lack of resources available to them, what a handful of guide-outfitters, trappers, biologists, and conservationists achieved for the area Leanne and I walked into next is nothing short of remarkable. Faced in the early 1990s with the opportunity to do something different with a chunk of fifty undeveloped watersheds, they proposed (and eventually got) a made-in-the-north solution that resulted in a block of protected areas and connecting corridors bigger than Switzerland.

For those who know the Y2Y proposal, the approach taken to establish the Muskwa-Kechika Management Area will sound familiar, and it should, for it was informed by the same science, which warns that lone protected areas are inadequate to conserve wide-ranging species. As a result, the multiyear, multijurisdictional planning process initiated by the New Democrat government and forwarded by northern residents and industry made conservation history in 1997: Twenty provincial parks covering 4 million acres were established, connected by an 11-million-acre system of Special Management Zones. Following the core-reserve-connecting-corridor model, the parks are off limits to development, while the Special Management Zones (a.k.a. wildlife corridors) allow for carefully controlled forestry and oil and gas activity where roads and infrastructure must be removed.

INTO THE BIG WILD

After a week of watching earth movers, tree cutters, and other oversize machinery ripping through the land, I was ready for a little wilderness-imposed humility, and it didn't take long for the roadless, bridgeless Muskwa-Kechika to deliver. Brimming with an estimated 4,000 caribou, 15,000 elk, 22,000 moose, 5,000 goats, 7,000 Stone sheep, and more predators than anyone knows, it more than lived up to its reputation as the Serengeti of North America. Within a few days of walking, Leanne and I were immersed in wildlife encounters: a wolverine lumbering within meters in an alpine meadow, another scaling a waterfall where we sat eating lunch, a curious caribou following for half an hour, grizzlies grazing around our tent as we slept, and face-to-face meetings with surprised packs of wolves. Between such moments we swam the glacier-fed rivers, waited out the storms, and did our best to traverse nameless valleys and high passes without getting lost. As days grew into weeks, and weeks into a month, the mental clutter gave way to the rhythm we'd only touched earlier that spring. It was the trails of grizzly bears, black bears, elk, caribou, wolves, deer, coyotes, caribou, and porcupines we followed now, not just wolverines, and with each footstep we felt a little more of the grace that had ended so abruptly with the mines and development around Tumbler Ridge.

It was deep within that flow, deep within our fifty-day traverse of the Muskwa-Kechika, that the power of big wilderness took hold. I was alone at the time, scouting a potential route while Leanne packed camp, when the moment I'd carefully avoided all trip confronted me. Coming up the canyon behind me was a large and determined bear.

It was a black bear, not a grizzly, but it didn't matter, for it had the claws, teeth, and power to injure or kill me, which seemed its intent. Unlike the dozens of bears we'd encountered in the months before, this one showed no timidity, shyness, or fear. Half-crouched and continuing its approach despite my shouts and arm-waves, it stalked me as a potential meal.

My outward reaction—rocks thrown, urine leaked, and profanities screamed—is less important than what happened inside. In the pinpoint of time where death hung in the balance, a sharp vitality took over, seconds stretched into minutes, and the textures, smells, and sights of the outer world moved within. Cold stone fused with fingers, ursid and human eyes connected, and with the babbling creek determining the tempo, an age-old dance played out. There were no houses to run to, no help to call for, no gun to draw. I had moved from the sidelines of life to the main playing field, and in the moment of reckoning, a sharp instinct picked up where the illusion of security and control left off.

When one of the fist-sized rocks connected with the bear's shoulder, it stopped and hesitated. I volleyed a whole new wave of stones and shouts in that pivotal moment, trying to wedge a crack of uncertainty into a rift of doubt. Another rock hit with a thud and the bear turned, looked back at me one last time, then fled. I stood there dazed for a few minutes, trying to orient myself in a future different from the death I'd already accepted. The pounding subsided in my chest, shaking legs grew quiet, and what had been a rich interlude in day-to-day living yielded back to the blunt edge of conventional time.

COMMITMENT TO PLACE

We were different people when we emerged from the fifty-day traverse of the Muskwa-Kechika, and part of me worried that as the trip came to a close, we would find ourselves returning to a world where we no longer fit. Fortunately, our first stop back in civilization was Lower Post, a Kaska Dena community straddling the British Columbia–Yukon border.

Unlike the Native American communities I'd visited farther south, Lower Post wasn't an Indian reservation, and it wasn't surrounded with development that had foreclosed all possibility of living from the land. As was the case with most (but not all) First Nations in the northern reach of Y2Y, recent or still-pending land claims ensured Native people the right to control natural resources within their traditional territories. For the Kaska, that meant hunting, fishing, and trapping in much of the Northern Rockies and southern Mackenzie Mountains. They had all the modern conveniences—a satellite dish was mounted on every stick-frame house, and inside the First Nation offices were computers hooked to the Internet—but as I was soon to find out, the people were different from the brash outdoorsmen and protective ranchers I'd met farther south. Forays into the surrounding wilderness weren't mere recreation. The Kaska were still deeply rooted to the land.

I had stood in front of hundreds of crowds before, but that night I was nervous as I got up to speak about Y2Y and show slides from the trip. Unlike many of the audiences I'd talked to in the towns and cities during the southern half of the trip, the chiefs and residents who had gathered in Lower Post's school gymnasium understood the cycles and needs of animals more deeply than I did. I consequently found myself glossing over the reasons behind Y2Y and homing in on what I'd seen instead. After touching on some of the key threats, I delivered my main message: In walking 2,100 miles (3,300 kilometers) from Yellowstone, I'd crossed only ten paved roads and five railways, and I had seen fresh sign of grizzly bears 85 percent of the way.

When the lights came up, not only did I see hope for Y2Y reflected back in every face, but soon I was inundated with people leading me to the maps taped to the wall.

"Here, this is where I still trap," said one man, brushing his brown, weathered hand over a corner of the paper. I glanced to where he pointed, an area west of where Leanne and I had hiked, but still days from any road. "I walk there too," he beamed.

"This is where my grandfather's trail runs," said a visiting chief from Ross River, Yukon. She was a small woman, and she could hardly reach the green curving lines toward the north end of the map. "We still hunt moose in those valleys every year."

More came after her, a whole string of people eager to talk about their own ties to the land, and in each one of them I sensed the humility and respect that I had only recently discovered. Because they lived surrounded by wilderness, and because they still walked into it, each one of them had his or her own story of an aggressive moose, a charging buffalo, or a marauding bear.

By the time the last of the people had left the gymnasium that night, I'd heard enough mention of "coming economic opportunities" to know a new era was about to start in Lower Post. As in every other place once considered remote, development now knocked on the Kaska Dena's door. Meetings with oil and gas companies had already started, and there was talk of beginning a small-scale forestry program soon. But when Leanne and I left the next morning and started walking the last few days into the Yukon, I was more comfortable than usual with the thought of environmental losses being weighed against economic gains. The difference wasn't in the value of the area—the Liard Basin where Lower Post sits is part of a critical link between the Rocky and Mackenzie mountains—but in the people doing the weighing. Unlike the faceless, calculating men from distant companies driving past Bruce Simpson's ranch, the Kaska—and their future families—would have to live with the consequences of their decisions. A poorly planned seismic line, for example, would lead wolves to a favorite moose hunting ground; washouts from roads and practices like clearcutting would ruin the spawning beds of the fish they netted each fall. The checks and balances between human and nonhuman residents were still intact with the Kaska Dena, and my hunch was that despite the challenges that lay ahead, that relationship would survive.

NO BOUNDARIES, NO END

We crossed the Yukon border and walked into the town of Watson Lake two days later, finishing on September 8, 1999, what had started in Yellowstone, Wyoming, 2,200 miles (3,500 kilometers) and eighteen months before. In that time, I'd seen enough grizzly bear sign and met enough conservation-minded people for a different geography to have taken form in my mind. Sure, there were problems—threats to wildlife movement as real and urgent in the north as they were in the south—but having walked the connections as well as the islands, and having seen fresh grizzly bear and wolverine sign 85 percent of the way, I knew that what was audacious was also possible. What had been a map of black dots, red lines, and green islands that might or might not be connected was now a geography of hope.

Snowflakes fell with the rain as we walked the last few miles into Watson Lake,

Stone sheep (Ovis dalli stonei) at *Muskwa-Kechika*, *British Columbia*

View of mountaintops by Tochodi Lakes in the Muskwa-Kechika

153

Left: Airplane taking off from Muncho Lake in Muskwa-Kechika, British Columbia. Above, left to right: Cooking over the campfire, outfitter style; horse trip with Wayne Sawchuck to explore the wildlands of the Muskwa-Kechika; Arctic grayling (Thymallus sp.)—*catch of the day*

and I thought of the 123,000 caribou gathering for the winter in the taiga forests at the northern tip of Y2Y. A part of me regretted not walking the final 600 (900 kilometers) miles to see such a spectacle, but to do so would have meant keeping going for at least another year. And even then the journey wouldn't have ended. No sooner would we have arrived among the caribou than they would have set off again, migrating north to their calving grounds, through Alaska's Brooks Range to the Arctic coast.

Like the grizzly bears, the wolverines, and every other wide-ranging mammal we'd followed, the caribou would tell us what our tired muscles and achy bones already knew: There are no boundaries to the Y2Y vision, no borders beyond which wildlife do or don't go.

But for Leanne and me there were limits. Too skinny and sore to keep going, we stopped for a short but welcome rest.

In 2003 Karsten Heuer and Leanne Allison continued their northern adventures, following the Porcupine Caribou herd from their Yukon winter range to their endangered Alaskan calving grounds and back.

KARSTEN HEUER

Trained as a biologist and recipient of the 2003 Wilburforce Foundation Conservation Leadership Award, Karsten Heuer has spent the better part of the last decade studying and, in some cases, actually following wide-ranging and threatened wildlife on foot. He has worked as a wildlife biologist and park warden in the Madikwe Game Reserve in South Africa, in Canada's Yukon Territory, and in Banff and Jasper national parks in the Canadian Rockies. Accompanied by his wife, Leanne Allison, and his border collie, he walked 2,200 miles (3,500 kilometers) from Yellowstone to the Yukon in 1998–99, and another 1,000 miles (1,600 kilometers) to Alaska's Arctic National Wildlife Refuge with the 123,000-member Porcupine Caribou herd in 2003. He is author of *Walking the Big Wild: From Yellowstone to the Yukon on the Grizzly Bear's Trail* and is currently writing his second book, *Being Caribou*. He lives with his wife and son near the base of Mount Robson in Dunster, British Columbia.

The Nahanni River, Northwest Territories

Right: The Selwyn Mountains, Northwest Territories

CANOEING THE NAHANNI RIVER.   After hours of flying over boreal forest, meandering streams, and the Mackenzie Mountains, we reached the Nahanni River, traditional territory of the Deh-Cho Dene Nation. Our bush pilot set us down on Island Lakes, then flew away, the noise ripping through the landscape like a chain saw. As the plane disappeared over the mountains, an eerie silence descended around us.

We portaged to the river and began our journey down the mysterious Nahanni. For days we didn't see another human being. But on every sandbank, we found evidence that we were not alone. On one bank was a large grizzly track accompanied by smaller prints—a grizzly family. Other banks were imprinted with the tracks of wolves, moose, black bear, and caribou. One day we spotted a wolf on a distant sandbank. We rested the paddles and drifted closer for a full view. The next day we came upon a grizzly feeding on berries. It reared back on its hind legs to get a better look at us, then turned and disappeared.

At Rabbitkettle Lake, we hiked up to the pools of Gahnihthah. Gahnihthah are tufa mounds with a central spring—a spot believed to be the birthplace of the Dene nation. Barefoot, we walked over the mounds. Following a tradition of the Deh-Cho Dene people, we stopped to look at the level of the water in the pools. If the pools are full, you will have a good journey. If they are empty, beware.

To our relief, the pools were full.

—F.S.

Clockwise from upper left: Grizzly bear (Ursus arctos) *tracks on the sandbanks of the Nahanni River; gray wolf* (Canis lupus) *against the tundra; camping along the Nahanni River; cold springs of the tufa mounds in the Rabbitkettle Lake area, Nahanni National Park; tufa mounds in the Rabbitkettle Lake area; canoeist paddling the Nahanni River (Photograph © by Emil Herrera Jara)*

Left: Paddling the Nahanni River, with the Cirque of the Unclimbables in the background, Northwest Territories

Canoeist paddling Virginia Falls on the Nahanni River, Northwest Territories (Photograph © by Emil Herrera Jara)

Right: Rabbitkettle Lake in Nahanni National Park, Northwest Territories, with the Logan Mountains in the background

The mountains around Macmillan Pass in the Mackenzie Mountains, Northwest Territories

Left: The Nahanni River, looking south from Virginia Falls, Nahanni National Park, Northwest Territories

Fall in the Mackenzie Mountains, Northwest Territories; caribou (Rangifer tarandus)

Right: Gray wolf (Canis lupus) *howling to its pack*

Mackenzie Mountains at Macmillan Pass, looking southwest into the the mountain range in Yukon Territory–Northwest Territories

DECHENLA:
LAND AT THE END OF THE TREES

Dave Porter

DECHENLA IS A WILD PLACE WHERE THE MOUNTAINS UNFOLD TO EMBRACE the land. Pristine peaks rising as high as 10,000 feet (3,000 meters) surround a plateau that is nearly 20 miles (32 kilometers) in diameter. Dechenla, or "Land at the End of the Trees," is a subarctic oasis with open tundra and alpine lakes in the traditional territory of the Kaska Dena. It is located just beyond the Yukon border in the Northwest Territories, surrounded by the Mackenzie and Selwyn Mountains. The region has been given special significance through the International Biological Program, indicating that scientists recognize it as a unique area because of its significant natural heritage.

I am a member of the Kaska Dena, one of Canada's remote indigenous groups. The Kaska are a group of five communities in northern British Columbia and the Yukon who govern themselves as a single nation. Our traditional territory consists of 93,000 square miles (240,870 square kilometers) of resource-rich land. It covers 25 percent of the Yukon, 10 percent of British Columbia, and adjacent lands in the Northwest Territories, including Dechenla.

The welfare of my people is inextricably linked to the land and animals that share it with us. We are constructing a Kaska Conservation Initiative to develop a conservation strategy for places like Dechenla and all of the Kaska Traditional Territory. We are attempting to learn from the bad decisions that have occurred in southern Canada and the Lower 48 states. Our efforts are founded on the principles of conservation that our people have always practiced.

Dechenla is a gathering place that has provided subsistence for people and animals for thousands of years. Biologists say more than 130 species of birds have been recorded at Dechenla. Visitors say this is a rare and magical place where the world still exists as it once was. In the summer months, four herds of mountain caribou walk this land in sight of moose, Dall sheep, wolves, grizzly bears, wolverines, and gyrfalcons.

For the Kaska Dena, Dechenla is an ancient spiritual place on the Dene Etene, or "the people's trail." The trail follows the natural corridor that runs from the Yukon to Yellowstone, a long stretch of land that binds all Dene together. It is believed that some Athapaskan ancestors left our northern land and traveled down the Dene Etene. Today, there are sixty groups of Athapaskan-speaking people in North America, including the Tutchone and the Sekani in Canada's North and the Apache and the Navajo in the United States.

Trails in the northern region of the Dene Etene remain an important part of aboriginal life. They provide access to hunting grounds, seasonal camps, and remote communities. In the Kaska Dena territory alone, the network of trails stretches over a thousand miles, from Kwadacha in British Columbia to Dechenla in the Northwest Territories.

The Kaska Dena and other northern subsistence-based indigenous groups, such as the Vuntut Gwich'in, who live in Old Crow, north of the Arctic Circle, are more fortunate than many of North America's aboriginal people. The land has provided for our people for millennia, and many still depend on wildlife for subsistence. We appreciate all that we have, and we view it as a sacred responsibility to care for the land and the animals that inhabit it. We must ensure that it will continue to provide for our people in the future as well as it has in the past.

Although we still enjoy an abundance of wildlife on our lands with a wealth of species, we listen with grave concern as elders and scientists tell us that some species in the south are at risk of extinction and many species are being sentenced to genetic islands that they can't escape. Transportation corridors, oil and gas fields, and mining interests continue to encroach on rare and wild spaces. We fear the effects

Grizzly bear (Ursus arctos) on the tundra, Northwest Territories

Left: Caribou in the high plateau of the Mackenzie Mountains, Northwest Territories

FIRST NATIONS AND NATIVE AMERICANS

Source: A Sense of Place: Issues, Attitudes, and Resources in the Yellowstone to Yukon Ecoregion. *Published by the Yellowstone to Yukon Conservation Initiative, 1998.*

The Y2Y region straddles the traditional territories of some thirty-one different Native American and First Nations tribes.

that development can have on our territory as industry marches north on a quest for resources. For us, conservation measures are imperative to ensure the longevity of all species and to maintain our traditional way of life.

There is a clear need to spark the ancient connection to the land once again, not only for the benefit of the Kaska Dena, but for all people. The tone and timbre of discussions about the future of development in this region must continue to be reframed and broadened to engage citizens, governments, industry, and organizations in a cooperative effort. Organizations must work together to maintain a wilderness that will allow wildlife to move freely across artificial political boundaries. Industry and government have extracted tremendous wealth out of the Rocky Mountains and the surrounding region, and they have an obligation to participate in efforts to protect our shrinking wild world.

The aboriginal people of North America have the potential to play a leadership role as this conservation dialogue unfolds. North America's indigenous people are the largest single private landowners in Canada and the United States. In northern

Canada alone, we own more than 250,000 square miles (647,500 square kilometers) of land, much of it with subsurface rights. That is an area as big as Alberta, bigger than California. Many northern land claim and treaty agreements have set aside large tracts of land for conservation purposes.

Our elders will guide us in our efforts to manage our lands. While some in scientific circles may still question the value of traditional knowledge, Kaska elders have repeatedly demonstrated the value of traditional knowledge in conservation planning efforts. For example, for years, Kaska elders told scientists about a particular area near Ross River, Yukon, that supported a healthy moose population. It was a place that could always be counted on to sustain our people. Recent government surveys have confirmed this assertion and revealed that this area has the highest densities of moose ever recorded in the Yukon. We strongly believe that traditional knowledge should be used in all land, wildlife, and resource planning efforts and be given an equal weight with scientific method.

While our elders' wisdom will guide our decisions, engaging youth in conservation efforts offers the greatest hope for long-term success. Many philosophies of the old ones are being taught to the young. Annual youth camps bring elders and biologists together at different sites throughout our traditional territory to share traditional and scientific knowledge with young people. Participants at a recent camp at Moose Lake, British Columbia, constructed a moose-skin boat—an art once feared lost that is now being rediscovered. We are willing to share our knowledge with others as well. In 2000 we hosted youth from seven foreign countries and twenty-two First Nations at a special Millennium Youth Camp on the Turnagain River in British Columbia. In addition to learning survival skills, participants learned how to make beadwork moccasins and how to make *súné' t'és*, often called bannock, a traditional flat bread, over an open fire.

Our conservation efforts will succeed. In fact, many significant contributions to conservation have been initiated by aboriginal people. Canada's indigenous people have insisted that most land claim agreements between First Nations and government have one or more special management areas where environmental and cultural values take precedence over development. Special management areas include national parks, national park reserves, national historic sites, migratory bird and wildlife sanctuaries, and watershed protection areas as well as other places where careful management is required. The objective with these areas is to maintain important features of the natural or cultural environment to benefit the public while respecting the rights of indigenous people.

Other Kaska Dena conservation efforts include negotiating a Memorandum of Understanding with the governments of Canada and the Yukon in 2002 that initiated an ecosystem-based forestry management process for a 42,470-square-mile (110,000-square-kilometer) region in the southeast Yukon.

Now it is our task to apply our skills and knowledge to conserve the valuable habitat in the much larger Yellowstone to Yukon region, as industrial encroachment continues to threaten some of North America's most important wild spaces.

For the Kaska Dena, conservation success will mean certainty that the plants and animals who share the land with us will thrive in the future, and that all people will be able to find a spiritual place in North America's shrinking wilderness.

Green moss growing over the stones of a marsh, Mackenzie Mountains, Northwest Territories

DAVE PORTER

Dave Porter is a Kaska Dena leader who spent his early years on a trapline near Good Hope Lake in British Columbia. His accomplished career includes journalism, politics, communications, and public service on behalf of Canadian aboriginal organizations as well as governments in the Yukon, British Columbia, and the Northwest Territories. He was founding chairman of Northern Native Broadcasting, Yukon, and was a two-term vice-chair of the Council for Yukon Indians. He has served as deputy premier of the Yukon and as assistant deputy Minister of Aboriginal Affairs for British Columbia. As the first Oil and Gas Commissioner in British Columbia, he strove to build an open regulatory environment that would bring various interests in the province to a common table. In 2004 he was elected to the First Nations Summit, which works on behalf of First Nations involved in the treaty negotiation process in British Columbia. He is committed to preserving indigenous culture and creating greater opportunity for aboriginal youth.

Plains of the Mackenzie Mountains, Northwest Territories

Kaska Natives on a caribou hunt in the high plateau of the Mackenzie Mountains, Northwest Territories; skinning the caribou; Dorothy Dicks, a Native Kaska woman, after hunting the caribou

CARIBOU HUNT.   I joined Kaska elder Hammond Dicks and his two daughters on a caribou hunt on the high-elevation plateau of Dechenla. It is one of the most stunning landscapes in the entire Y2Y region. The plains stretch toward the horizon, stopping abruptly at the distant mountain peaks. Grizzlies, wolves, wolverines, ptarmigan, golden eagles, and gyrfalcons thrive here, and every fall, herds of caribou migrate south across the plains.

From a small hill, we could see caribou in the far distance, dwarfed to the size of ants by the enormous landscape. Dick spotted a group of bulls grazing nearby. We crept within range, crawling across the tundra, inhaling the fresh, moist smell of lichen and moss. The two daughters selected one animal and took it together, one shot each.

The Kaska have hunted on this plateau for millennia, practicing one of humankind's most ancient rituals. They hunt for food, not for sport. What few remains Hammond and his daughters left on the plains after skinning and quartering the bull would quickly be consumed by a grizzly or wolverine.

There is hope and there are threats to this incredible landscape and its wildlife. Plans are in the works for building the biggest tungsten mine in the western world. But there are also plans for protecting the area, keeping it a place where Native groups still can go about their traditional hunts. The struggle continues.   —F.S.

The Tombstone Range after a snowstorm, Tombstone Range Provincial Park, Yukon Territory

Right: Northern hawk owl (Surnia ulula)

The northern lights in Tombstone Range Provincial Park, Yukon Territory

The vision of the Yellowstone to Yukon Conservation Initiative (Y2Y)—*people working together to ensure that the world-renowned wilderness, wildlife, native plants, and natural processes of the Yellowstone to Yukon region continue to function as an interconnected web of life, capable of supporting all of the natural and human communities that reside within it, for now and for future generations*—has come a very long way in a very short time. Since 1993 the effort to realize a unified ecosystem linked from one end of the region to the other has grown from a simple idea to an ongoing movement that is already making significant differences in the protection of wildlife habitats and movement corridors and in the ways that people think about their role in caring for the land.

People working together: Those three words are essential to the continuing realization of the Yellowstone to Yukon dream. It began with scientific researchers developing a clear understanding of what is at stake in this astonishing region. "Look at the populations of fourteen key carnivores and ungulates and you'll find that the only place left in North America with a high density of all those species is Y2Y," explains Rob Buffler, executive director of the Yellowstone to Yukon Conservation Initiative. "The science is helping us understand the continental significance of the landscape."

Scientific studies have identified critical core habitats and linkage corridors that require protection and innovative management to preserve the spectacular ecological diversity that unifies Y2Y and defines its innate wildness. From the Greater Yellowstone Ecosystem north through the Salmon-Selway-Bitterroot Mountains, the Northern Continental Divide Ecosystem, the Canadian Rocky Mountain parks complex, and the Muskwa-Kechika all the way to the wild expanses of the Yukon and the Northwest Territories, researchers are making remarkable progress in designing practical proposals that will help advance protection and management goals.

We are now past defining vision and well into the second phase of Yellowstone to Yukon, that of encouraging individuals, organizations, foundations, and governments to engage in the actual work of making proposals realities by safeguarding critical habitat, establishing wildlife movement corridors, and completing a multitude of other stewardship projects that will have a lasting impact on the quality of this continental-scale "wildlife highway" that is the Y2Y bioregion.

There have already been many successes on the ground, including the construction of wildlife road-crossing structures, the establishment of new parks, the designation of special management areas on public lands, and certification of some sustainable forestry areas. In places like Montana and Alberta's Rocky Mountain Front, private landowners working with land trusts are finding ways to ensure that their properties remain wildlife-friendly. Larger-scale efforts are under way, as well. For example, the Yellowstone to Yukon Conservation Initiative worked with Nature Conservancy of Canada and the forestry company Tembec, Inc., to secure almost 173 square miles (450 square kilometers) of forested private lands in the Elk and Flathead valleys, allowing wildlife to move more freely through portions of southeastern British Columbia and southwestern Alberta. Strongly supported by the East Kootenay Environmental Society (now Wildsight), the Canadian Parks and Wilderness Society, the Montana Chapter of The Nature Conservancy, and donors from across the continent, the acquisition represents the biggest private conservation project of its kind ever undertaken in Canada.

Public interest and involvement in Y2Y has been encouraged by many gifted and committed individuals. Spurred on by American conservationist Ernest LaBelle, the National Geographic Society in 2000 published Douglas Chadwick's *Yellowstone to Yukon,* the first book on the Y2Y vision. Canadian park warden and biologist Karsten

Y2Y Today
Where We Are and Where We Go from Here
Harvey Locke and Gary Tabor

Full moon rising over the Mackenzie Mountains at Macmillan Pass, Northwest Territories

Left: Northern lights in Tombstone Range Provincial Park, Yukon Territory

Heuer walked from Yellowstone to the Yukon and in 2004 produced a book of his own—*Walking the Big Wild: From Yellowstone to the Yukon on the Grizzly Bear's Trail.* Other foot travelers, including Walkin' Jim Stoltz and Josh Burnim, have journeyed through significant portions of the Y2Y landscape, then brought their stories and songs to classrooms and community gatherings throughout the region. Grade school teachers and college professors alike are including the Y2Y concept in their courses. Several doctoral dissertations and a number of masters' theses have focused attention on issues surrounding Y2Y. Local, national, and international media have featured the Yellowstone to Yukon idea.

A crucial aspect of the Yellowstone to Yukon Conservation Initiative is the understanding that the well-being of the people of the region is interconnected with the health and vitality of the land and its wild creatures. First Nations and Native Americans have always known this and are increasingly sharing their wisdom and taking an active role in the management of the region for the benefit of all species. In Wyoming the Shoshone tribe has established the Wind River Alliance to coordinate the efforts of conservation groups improving the water quality of the Wind River Watershed. In the Northwest Territories, the Deh Cho First Nations are supporting a major expansion of Nahanni National Park, and in British Columbia the Kaska Tribal Council and members of the Kaska Dena have been key to the creation and protection of the Muskwa-Kechika Management Area. In northern Canada, the Deh Cho, Kaska Dena, and Tetl'it Gwich'in First Nations are turning the Y2Y vision into reality by striving to build successful, vibrant communities and economies on principles of conservation planning that protect and connect critical wildlife habitats.

Under the umbrella of the Yellowstone to Yukon Conservation Initiative, a host of conservation groups, businesses, scientists, and other advocates are assembling the pieces of the Yellowstone to Yukon puzzle. The Y2Y network today includes more than 200 nonprofit organizations, business, and charitable foundations, about evenly split between those in the United States and those in Canada. Working cooperatively, they are supporting one another's ventures and learning from their successes how the efforts of everyone across the region can contribute to the whole.

Ensuring the ecological integrity of an area so immense and diverse may seem daunting, but there are precedents for success. The establishment of Yellowstone National Park in 1872 was a revolutionary concept for its time, as was the formation of Banff National Park a few years later. With the creation of Waterton-Glacier International Peace Park in 1932, Canada and the United States recognized that political borders are meaningless to Nature. Those leading examples of setting aside lands for the sake of wildlife and of present and future generations have influenced the formation of the many more parks, designated wilderness areas, and other protected lands not only in the Yellowstone to Yukon region but also around the world.

In many cases, the boundaries of those protected areas were drawn without a full understanding or acknowledgment of the greater ecosystem surrounding and ultimately connecting the many islands of wildlands. If we have learned anything from wildlife, it is that lines on a map mean nothing. Animals and plants do not distinguish between protected and unprotected lands—there is simply the place where they live. For many species, that home stretches from Yellowstone to the Yukon.

The challenges for conserving the ecosystem of the Y2Y region are immense, filled with opportunities for individuals and organizations to educate one another, share ideas, and seek out solutions. It will take at least one lifetime, and perhaps several, before the goals of Y2Y are fully realized, but the vision is in place, and the momentum necessary to continue has been developed. Across the entire region, people are applying their talents and energies with tremendous enthusiasm, secure in the knowledge that they are engaged in an effort that is truly important, possible to achieve, and of great value today and for generations to come.

The website of the Yellowstone to Yukon Conservation Initiative (*www.y2y.net*) contains a wealth of information for individuals, organizations, and foundations that want to help advance the vision of Y2Y. Here are some possibilities:

- Visit the website and join the Yellowstone to Yukon Conservation Initiative. Monetary contributions provide a tremendous boost for programs designed to maintain one of the world's most cherished mountain environments.
- Stay informed about current issues through Y2Y links to publications, and take action on issues that concern you. Your connection to Y2Y helps sustain the landscape connection of the Y2Y region.
- Volunteer time, energy, and ideas. More than 200 organizations, businesses, and charitable foundations are actively involved in forwarding the vision of Y2Y. Many have opportunities for volunteers to help with projects.

Just as Yellowstone and Banff national parks have served as benchmarks in the preservation of wildlands, Y2Y is a beacon of what is possible for the protection of ecosystems that encompass far more than a few designated parks and forests. The beginnings of other conservation initiatives around the world (Baja to Bering in the Eastern Pacific, Algonquin to Adirondacks in eastern North America, the Trans-Limpopo effort in southern Africa, the Gondwana Link in Australia, and the Cantabric-Pyrenees-Alps Initiative in southern Europe, to name a few) resonate with the energy and success of the Y2Y vision. Yellowstone to Yukon is an idea whose time has come, and a testament to the power of a vision when people apply knowledge, initiative, and their hearts to creating a better future.

International Mountain Corridor Conference participants at Waterton-Glacier International Peace Park, Alberta

© Wendy Francis

HARVEY LOCKE

Harvey Locke grew up in southern Alberta. His family, among the area's earliest European settlers, has been in Bow Valley for seven generations. Locke first visited Yellowstone in 1979 and knew intuitively there was a connection between it and the Canadian Rockies. This interest led him to help create the Yellowstone to Yukon Conservation Initiative, for which he now serves as strategic advisor. He also serves as program advisor to Tides Canada Foundation; senior advisor, conservation, to the Canadian Parks and Wilderness Society; advisor to the Canadian Boreal Initiative; director emeritus of the Wildlands Project; member of the World Commission on Protected Areas; member of the executive committee of the Eighth World Wilderness Congress; and trustee of the Eleanor Luxton Historical Foundation. In 1999 *Time* Canada magazine named him one of Canada's leaders for the twenty-first century.

© Raina Plowright

GARY TABOR

Gary Tabor is the head of Wilburforce Foundation's Bozeman, Montana, office and its Yellowstone to Yukon Program, which promotes science and conservation to maintain ecological connectivity between parks and protected areas in the U.S. and Canadian Rocky Mountains. He was trained as a wildlife veterinarian and ecologist. His career spans international and North American wildlife conservation domains, including seven years in East Africa and one year in South America. After helping to establish several protected areas abroad, Tabor was asked by his African colleagues to name any of his successes back home. This epiphany led to his catalytic involvement in helping to transform the Y2Y vision from theory to reality—first as associate director of the Henry P. Kendall Foundation in 1995 and now with Wilburforce.

Mount McKinley at dawn, reflected in Wonder Lake, Denali National Park, Alaska

Rainbow over the tundra, Denali National Park, Alaska

Muskoxen (Ovibos moschatus) *on the Arctic Plains, Alaska. Left: The Brooks Range, Alaska*

INTO ALASKA. It was the first days of September. Fall had come and gone on the tundra: an explosion of color that all too soon faded to a dull brown. Following the fall colors, we would make our way south again, but not before crossing into Alaska.

We were driving along the Top of the World Highway, toward the Alaska–Yukon border, surrounded by incredible views of mountain ranges. In the far distance I spotted the Alaska Range, with mighty Mount McKinley standing proud. Between us and the continent's tallest peak stretched miles of undisturbed mountains and valleys.

This immense, unobstructed view into Alaska made me reflect on the nature of "borders." Borders have significance only for humans; for nature, they mean nothing. Wildlife habitat and migration patterns are not defined by country, province, or state borders, nor by the borders of parks or preserves. And Y2Y does not stop at a border either. Like the Yukon River and the timeless migration of the caribou, the Y2Y region flows across the Yukon border into Alaska. Vast, primitive Alaska—another vein bringing sustenance and energy into the interconnected web of life that is Y2Y.

—F.S.

Epilogue

Robert F. Kennedy Jr.

THE STUNNINGLY BEAUTIFUL PHOTOGRAPHS OF FLORIAN SCHULZ CONTAINED in this book, as well as these marvelous essays, bring to life one of the biggest and most spectacular wild places in North America: the mountainous backbone of the continent that is the Yellowstone to Yukon region. This natural garden of Eden is home to a vast array of living beings. It is a refuge for species such as the wolf, grizzly, and trumpeter swan that have been eliminated or drastically reduced elsewhere. At its heart is wilderness, a resource that enriches humanity and has played a particularly critical role in defining the culture and national character of both Canada and the United States. David Suzuki reminds us that wilderness links us to a unique spiritual legacy, to the seasons and the tides and the 10,000 generations of human beings who lived before laptops.

Europeans destroyed the last of their wilderness 1,000 years ago. But in the United States and Canada, we have managed to preserve some vestiges, such as those illuminated on these pages, thanks to leaders who recognized our strong cultural and historical connections to wilderness. Out of our wilderness experience we grew in self-reliance, physical courage, and fortitude. Following the close of the frontier 100 years ago, concern mounted that Americans would lose those traits and become soft. This fear led Teddy Roosevelt to re-create himself as a frontiersman; it also drove President John F. Kennedy to climb Mount Kennedy, the tallest unclimbed peak in the Canadian Rockies, and take our family hiking in national parks and paddling on white-water rivers. He saw these adventures as frontier metaphors that allowed us to struggle with nature without destroying it.

Today the challenge of living with wild nature without harming what we love is crystallized in the battle over the future of the Yellowstone to Yukon region. Here, even in what appears to be some of the most remote country in the continent, the pace of development is escalating. As several authors in this book point out, we now know that the parks and wilderness areas are too small and isolated to maintain the wildlife they were intended to protect.

This comes at a time when new technologies, combined with aggressive energy development on both sides of the 49th parallel, are turning the last habitat for bighorn sheep, wolves, and trout into industrialized zones with pipelines, pump stations, and oil rigs. Whole mountaintops are being removed to dig coal not far from Waterton Lakes and Jasper National Parks. Ancient forests are being clearcut, and habitat for wildlife that has nowhere else to go is being destroyed. Native trout populations are collapsing as a result of dams and water developments.

Why is this happening? Because the governments of both Canada and the United States are dominated by large corporations that are driven to maximize short-term profits at the expense of the interests of future generations. Massive governmental subsidies to energy, lumber, mining, and agribusiness companies–with some of the largest subsidies occurring in the West–are driving the destruction of the last remaining wild places such as the Y2Y region.

To enrich a wealthy few, both nations' governments are borrowing from our children, poisoning our water and air, destroying our public lands, and sacrificing our health. No place is exempt from this exploitation. Not the wilderness that shaped our culture, not Yellowstone, our nation's oldest national park, not the magnificent Canadian mountain parks. Not the last few grizzly bears hanging on by a thread in the Lower 48 and Alberta.

Here, in the wild heart of North America, we must take a stand. We must stand firm on the principle of wilderness that has shaped our identity and spirit. We must stand up for wild creatures that have no voice in government. We must stand and fight against the forces of short-term profit over the interests of future generations. We must also learn to live by the wisdom expressed on these pages about how to coexist respectfully and humbly with wild nature. We must put into action the scientific understanding described here of how to maintain natural corridors between ecosystems.

If we are to prevail, no one can sit on the sidelines. The pressures are mounting, and the window of opportunity is closing rapidly. Faced with such powerful forces for development, we must find new ways of working together, each and every one of us, contributing what we can to make this vision of a connected wildland complex from the Yellowstone to the Yukon a reality.

This means making all the tools of democracy work: Protesting and litigating harmful proposals and efforts to roll back environmental laws. Passing legislation to protect new parks and wilderness areas. Working with First Nations and Native American tribes to sustain their cultural traditions and preserve the land and wildlife upon which they depend. Buying lands for conservation purposes. Developing new initiatives at the local level to keep our water and air clean and the wildlife and human communities healthy. Taking back the political process. This will require courage, a commitment to community, and a willingness to make sacrifices on behalf of future generations.

If we fail and allow these last wild places to be destroyed, we will diminish ourselves and impoverish our children. If we succeed, we will give the world an example of what conservation can mean, which will be as significant for our time as the establishment of national parks were more than a century ago.

Reflections of last light on Kluane Lake, Kluane National Park, Yukon Territory

ROBERT F. KENNEDY JR.

ROBERT F. KENNEDY JR. has worked on environmental issues across the Americas. He was named one of *Time* magazine's "Heroes for the Planet" for his success in helping Riverkeeper lead the fight to restore the Hudson River. The watershed agreement he negotiated on behalf of environmentalists and New York City watershed consumers is regarded as an international model in stakeholder consensus negotiations and sustainable development. Kennedy serves as senior attorney for the Natural Resources Defense Council, chief prosecuting attorney for the Hudson Riverkeeper, and president of Waterkeeper Alliance. Among his published books are *Crimes Against Nature* and *The Riverkeepers*. His articles have appeared in, among others, *The New York Times, Washington Post, Los Angeles Times, Wall Street Journal, Newsweek, Rolling Stone, Atlantic Monthly, Esquire, The Nation, Outside,* and the *Village Voice*. Kennedy is a licensed master falconer, and as often as possible he pursues a life-long enthusiasm for white-water paddling.

Photographer's Notes

Red fox (Vulpes vulpes) *catching a young white-fronted goose* (Anser albifrons), *Arctic Plains, Alaska*

I **STARTED TAKING PHOTOGRAPHS AT THE AGE OF TWELVE. I STILL REMEMBER** lying on my belly, taking pictures of a small lizard with a manual Praktika camera and 200mm lens. I've been hooked on photography ever since. It has become my deep passion.

For me, photography is about being in the natural world, experiencing the landscape and wildlife firsthand and telling that story. I also hope to inspire in viewers a desire to conserve and protect those wild spaces. I always photograph wildlife in their natural habitats, never on game farms. Also, all the photographs in this book were shot on film, not with digital cameras. It's true that with today's technology, a person can sit at a computer and create a fake digital image—but what story can a faked image tell?

With both landscape and wildlife photography, I've found that I must use my imagination to envision what *could* be there, even if I can't see it at the moment. On a gray day, a landscape may not look like much. But if I imagine the possibility of light breaking through the clouds to highlight certain features, I'll be there if it happens. I also keep myself constantly aware of north, south, west, and east, so I know how the light will fall. In this book, you will notice images that have a very strong blue cast. That is the natural blue light of dusk and dawn, which I like to capture for atmosphere.

Simple determination is essential to successful wildlife and landscape photography. When it is cold and wet outside and the alarm clock rips you out of a sweet dream, your lazier self tells you to stay in the warm sleeping bag. But you need to get out there, even if you have been out there a hundred times and nothing has happened. A mix of clouds, rain, and sun can result in an incredible shot. To photograph wildlife, you need to return to the same place over and over again, to learn the patterns of the animals and to recognize individuals. I often try to put myself into the animal's mind and anticipate certain movements, so I can be a step ahead and capture the actual scene. (That is how I got the shots of a fox catching a goose that you see on these pages.) A unique shot is unique for a reason: It does not happen every day.

My 35mm equipment consists of Nikon F5, F100, F 90, and FM-2 cameras, with the following lenses: AF-I 500mm f4, AF-S 200–400mm f4 VR, AF-S 300mm f2.8, AF-S 70–200mm f2.8, 105mm f2.8 macro, 28–70mm f3.5–4.5, AF-S 17–35mm f2.8, 20mm f2.8. For underwater photography, I use a Nikonos V with a 20mm f2.8 lens. In ten years no camera or lens has ever quit working, despite constant use.

To capture the vastness of a landscape, I work with a Fuji GX 617 panorama camera, with 105mm f8 and 180mm f6.7 lenses. When space and weight was a problem, I use a Hasselblad Xpan panorama camera with the 45mm and 90mm lenses. The Xpan is a beautiful and very versatile camera. I also use a manual Pentax 645, with 200mm f4, 75mm f2.8, 55mm f2.8, 45mm f2.8, and 35mm f3.5 lenses. I mount cameras and lenses on a Gitzo tripod.

My 35mm film consists primarily of Fuji Velvia 50 and Fuji Sensia 100, as well as some Provia 100 and 400, especially for the northern lights. For larger formats, I use Kodak 100 VS next to Velvia 50. When film can't bridge the contrast of several stops of light, I used 1-, 2-, or 3-stop neutral density filters to capture the scene as the human eye would see it.

I'm often asked how I transport all of my camera equipment. When I go on a trip that involves air travel, I pack all the gear into a hard-shell Pelican case. When I reach my destination, I repack my gear into Lowepro Trekker backpacks, which are very comfortable to carry without being bulky. Obviously, I can't carry all of my camera equipment out into the field. Therefore, I decide beforehand whether to concentrate on landscape photography or on wildlife. If I am going out on a predominantly wildlife shoot, I pack telephoto lenses and then squeeze in the Hasselblad Xpan to capture any interesting panoramic scenes.

While the right equipment is very important, it is still just a tool. Living in these digital times, when everything is becoming increasingly technical, we must not forget that true wildlife and landscape photography is about being out there. I hope to see you in the field some day!

(To learn more about my work, please visit my website *www.visionsofthewild.com.*)

—*Florian Schulz*

Y2Y Resources

THE Y2Y PARTNERSHIP NETWORK

More than 200 organizations, businesses, and foundations have joined together in the Yellowstone to Yukon conservation effort. Hand in hand, they are making the Yellowstone to Yukon vision become a reality in our communities and on the landscape. Learn how to get involved in these organizations by contacting the Y2Y Conservation Initiative.

YELLOWSTONE TO YUKON CONSERVATION INITIATIVE

In Canada:
1240 Railway Avenue, Unit 200
Canmore, Alberta T1W 1P4
(T) 403-609-2666
(F) 403-609-2667
info@y2y.net
In the United States:
503 W. Mendenhall Street
Bozeman, MT 59715
(T) 406-582-7840
(F) 406-586-4700
www.y2y.net

INTERNATIONAL

Earthjustice
Environmental Investigation Agency
McDonough Braungart Design Chemistry
Natural Resources Defense Council
Native Forest Network
Round River Conservation Studies
Ursus International
The Wildlands Project
William McDonough and Partners

CANADIAN NATIONAL/REGIONAL

Animal Alliance of Canada
Canadian Nature Federation
Canadian Parks and Wilderness Society (CPAWS)
Defenders of Wildlife Canada
Into the Wild
Western Canada Wilderness Committee
Wildcanada.net
Wildlands League
World Wildlife Fund - Canada

ALBERTA

Alberta Wilderness Association
Aspen Wildlife Research
Banff Centre/ Mountain Culture
BEAR Society
Bow Valley Grizzly Bear Alliance
Bow Valley Naturalists
BowCORD
Bragg Creek Environmental Coalition
Castle-Crown Wilderness Coalition
Central Rockies Wolf Project

CPAWS Calgary/Banff
CPAWS Edmonton
Crowsnest Environmental Action Society
Eastern Slopes Grizzly Bear Project
Federation of Alberta Naturalists
Freshwater Research Limited
Friends of Banff National Park
Friends of the Whaleback
Geoworks
Great Divide Nature Interpretation
Jasper Environmental Association
Lafarge
Miistakis Institute for the Rockies
Mountain Gate Community School
Mountain Parks Watershed Association
Orex Engineering Ltd
Pembina Institute for Appropriate Development
Precipice Theatre Society
Red Deer River Naturalists
Sierra Club of Canada Chinook Group
Sierra Club Prairie Chapter
Southern Alberta Environmental Group
Trail of the Great Bear Society
Trout Unlimited Canada
UTSB Research
West Athabaska Bioregional Society
Wolf Awareness Inc.

BRITISH COLUMBIA

Applied Conservation GIS
Applied Ecological Stewardship Council of BC
BC Endangered Species Coalition
BC Spaces for Nature
Cariboo-Chilcotin Conservation Council
Carswell Productions
Chetwynd Environmental Society
Columbia Mountains Institute of Applied Ecology
Columbia Valley Field Naturalists
CPAWS BC
Earth Wild International
East Kootenay Environmental Society (Wildsight)
  Wildsight—Elk Valley
  Wildsight—Golden
  Wildsight—Invermere
  Wildsight—Kimberley/Cranbrook
Fernie Nature Tours

Fraser Headwaters Alliance
Friends of Mount Revelstoke and Glacier
Friends of the Columbia Wetlands
Friends of the Granby Environmental Society
Friends of the Stikine Society
Geomar Consulting
Global Forest Science
Granby Wilderness Society
Harrop-Procter Watershed Protection Society
J.J. Whistler Bear Society/Canadian Bear Alliance
Jumbo Creek Conservation Society
The Land Conservancy of British Columbia—Kootenay Area Office
Osprey Communications
Peace Habitat and Conservation Endowment Trust
Planet Earth EcoRegion Society
Rockies Institute Society
Quesnel River Watershed Alliance
Save-The-Cedar League
Shuswap Environmental Action Society
Sierra Club of British Columbia
Silva Forest Foundation
Skyline Images
Turtle Island Earth Stewards
Valhalla Wilderness Society
West Kootenay Coalition for Jumbo Wild
West Kootenay Community EcoSociety

NORTHWEST TERRITORIES

CPAWS NWT

YUKON

CPAWS Yukon
Friends of Yukon Rivers
Yukon Conservation Society

UNITED STATES NATIONAL/REGIONAL

Advocates for the West
American Lands
American Wildlands
Audubon Expedition Institute
Biodiversity Conservation Alliance
Defenders of Wildlife USA
Ducks Unlimited
Endangered Species Coalition
Grassroots Environmental Effectiveness Network

Great Bear Foundation
Greater Yellowstone Coalition
Humane Society of U.S. Northern Rockies Regional Office
Musicians United to Sustain the Environment
National Network of Forest Practitioners
National Parks Conservation Association
Predator Conservation Alliance
Rocky Mountain Elk Foundation
Sonoran Institute
Training Resources for the Environmental Community
The Vital Ground Foundation
Watershed Consulting LLC
Wild Way
The Wilderness Society
Wilderness Watch
Wildlands Center for Preventing Roads

IDAHO

Clearwater Biodiversity Project
Cove Mallard Coalition
Earthfire Institute
Ecosystem Sciences Foundation
Friends of the Clearwater
Idaho Conservation League
Idaho Rivers United
Kootenai Environmental Alliance
LTB Consulting
Rock Creek Alliance
Selkirk Conservation Alliance
Valley Advocates for Responsible Development
Winter Wildlands Alliance
Wolf Education and Research Center Foundation

MONTANA

Big Sky Conservation Institute
Brown Bear Resources
Buffalo Field Campaign
Cabinet-Yaak Forest Coalition
Clancy-Unionville Citizens' Task Force
Clark Fork Coalition
Conservation Land Network
Craighead Environmental Research Institute
Deer Lodge Conservation Coalition
Deer Lodge Forest Defense Fund
Ecology Center

Forest Stewards Guild—Northern Rockies Chapter
Friends of the Bitterroot
Friends of the Rocky Mountain Front
Friends of the Wild Swan
Great Burn Study Group
Montana Environmental Information Center
Montana Trout Unlimited
Montana Wetlands Legacy
Montana Wilderness Association
Montana Wildlife Federation
National Wildlife Federation
Northern Rockies Project Office
Northwest Connections
Outlandish Real Estate
PR Media Consultants
Sierra Club Grizzly Bear Ecosystems Project
Southwest Montana Wildlands Alliance
Sustainability Fund
Swan Ecosystem Center
Swan View Coalition
Turner Endangered Species Fund
Whitebark Pine Ecosystem Foundation
Wild Rockies Earth First!
Wild Rockies Field Institute
Wild Things Unlimited
Wildlife Conservation Society
Women's Voices for the Earth
Yellowstone Safari Company

OREGON

Hell's Canyon Preservation Council

WASHINGTON

Conservation Biology Center
The Lands Council
Northwest Ecosystem Alliance

WYOMING

Audubon Wyoming
Jackson Hole Chamber of Commerce
Jackson Hole Conservation Alliance
Jackson Hole Land Trust
Jackson Hole Wildlife Foundation
Northern Rockies Conservation Cooperative
Upper Green River Valley Coalition
Wyoming Outdoor Council
Wyoming Wildlife Federation

Acknowledgments

A PROJECT OF THIS MAGNITUDE CANNOT BE COMPLETED ALONE. I AM DEEPLY indebted to the many people who have provided the support and assistance necessary to make this book a reality.

First, I thank my loving parents, Gerdi and Achim Schulz. They raised me with a curiosity for the world, and they have supported me beyond belief. My siblings, Jonathan, Immanuel, Sarah, and Salomon, have stood behind me and helped me whenever they could. And my partner, Emil Herrera Jara, has been by my side throughout most of this project, providing invaluable support through some of the hardest times. I've appreciated beyond words her dedication and assistance, in both the field and the office.

When I first came to this continent as an exchange student, Barbara Field and John and Kathy Albertini welcomed me into their homes. More recently, Teri and Brad Poindexter and their daughter, Jenny, have accepted me as part of their family and provided me with a home away from home for more than ten years. And many thanks to Art Wolfe, who welcomed me to his house whenever I was in Seattle.

This project picked up tremendous momentum once I connected with people in Seattle. The initial link was Joel Connelly, an outstanding journalist at the *Seattle Post-Intelligencer* who has been consistently supportive and encouraging. Joel put me in touch with Tom and Sonya Campion, who have become tremendous supporters. Tom introduced me to Helen Cherullo, publisher at The Mountaineers Books, who has been wonderful to work with; her vision for "Mission Publishing" is truly inspirational.

Thanks to The Mountaineers Books staff for their tireless efforts to transform the ideas and vision for this book into the final product: editors Deb Easter, Joan Gregory, and Linda Gunnarson; director of editorial and production Kathleen Cubley; designer Ani Rucki; publicist Alison Koop, and director of sales and marketing Doug Canfield.

Special thanks to the writers who have given this book such a strong and authentic voice. In countless ways, all were supportive with ideas, leads, information, and encouragement: Rick Bass, Douglas Chadwick, Karsten Heuer, Robert Kennedy Jr., Ted Kerasote, Harvey Locke, Dave Porter, David Quammen, David Suzuki (and his executive assistant, Elois Yaxley), and Gary Tabor. Also, for writing support, thanks to Robert Birkby and Celia Sollows. The folks at the Yellowstone to Yukon Conservation Initiative provided invaluable assistance and advice: Rob Buffler, Jeff Gailus, Rowan Hill, Brian Horesji, Cynthia Lane, Mike Matz, Bob Peart, Marlis Strebel, and Christine Torgrimson, among others.

My sincere thanks go to Blue Earth Alliance for playing a key role in making this Y2Y project happen. Many thanks to Judy DeBarros, Malcolm Edwards, Anna Farr, Natalie Fobes, Kristin Ianniciello, and Adam L. Weintraub. Subhankar Banerjee provided me with valuable advice from his own experiences as well as moral support.

This project would not have been possible without the people and foundations that have so generously sponsored it: the Y2Y Conservation Initiative; Jennifer Goethals, Tim Greyhavens, and Gary Tabor and the Wilburforce Foundation; Martha Kongsgaard and the Kongsgaard-Goldman Foundation; the Seattle Foundation; Erik Schultz and the Arthur B. Schultz Foundation; and the United States Trust Company of New York. I also am grateful to the folks at the Natural Resources Defense Council, especially Susan Casey-Lefkowitz, Jacob Scherr, and Louisa Willcox.

Many other conservation groups assisted me greatly and helped me develop contacts: The Nature Conservancy, especially Melissa Ryan and Tana Kappel from the TNC Montana office; the Greater Yellowstone Coalition; the Montana Wilderness Association; the Canadian Parks and Wilderness Society, especially Dave Poulton; the National Parks Conservation Association, especially Steve Thompson; the Predator Conservation Alliance, in particular Janelle Holden and range-rider Ebby Kunesh; Lance Craighead and the Craighead Environmental Research Institute; Dave Ausband with the Swift Fox Project; and Wayne Sawchuk, who is on the advisory board of the Muskwa-Kechika Management Area and a board member of the Y2Y Conservation Initiative.

While traveling the Y2Y region all those years, I met many wonderful people who have become good friends: fellow photographer Mark Miller, writers Linda and Alex Harker, painter Lyn St. Clair, filmmaker Jeff Hogan, Christiane and Dale Sekora, Marian and Robin White, Julia and Dustin Lynx, and pilot Håkon Askerhaug. Thank you all for great conversations and your friendship. My deep respect and gratitude go to Karl Rappold, a true conservationist who has fought major conservation battles on the Rocky Mountain Front. Thank you, Karl and Terri, for sharing your home and your time.

Sincere thanks to the many members of Native communities who have worked with me, including Steven Small Salmon of the Salish-Kootenay tribe, Bob Black Bull and Leon Rattler of the Blackfeet, and Richard Old Coyote of the Crow. While traveling in the Mackenzie Mountains, I had wonderful encounters with Native Kaska-Dena, who, for example, shared with us their fresh caribou meat. Kaska leader Dave Porter invited us to stay at Dechenla during the annual gathering of elders. Hammond and Dorothy Dick allowed me to join them on their caribou hunt. Thanks to Peter Stone for a ride in his truck and to Barb and Norm Barichello for wonderful meals and shelter at the Dechenla interpretive natural history lodge. Thanks also to Bill Lux, John Ward, and many others and to George Smith for putting us in touch.

And finally, I'm deeply grateful to the many friends, fellow photographers, and fellow conservationists who have helped in countless ways: Renate Schreieck; Steven Kazlowski and Sunny Coulson; Brooke T. Boswell; Gavriel Jeacan, who provided me a place to stay in Seattle; John Cornforth; Christina Mittermeier; Bettina Ginther of Farbglanz Imaging; Pam Voth and Rob Whitehair; and Ulf, Sylvia and Helga Steinmann.

Many other people have been a part of my life and this project over the past years. I thank you all. This book would have been impossible without you.

—*Florian Schulz*

Index